SYSTEMATIC GOLF

A Complete Golf Instruction Course

SYSTEMATIC GOLF

A Complete Golf Instruction Course

Mike Palmer

Sterling Publishing Co., Inc.   New York

A special thank you to those who have assisted me in this project,
most notably Colin Callander, Editor of *Golf Monthly* magazine,
Harro Peetoom, my photographic model, Keith Hailey for his golf
photography expertise and Greg Dukart, Head Golf Professional at
East Sussex National Golf Club, England. Thank you to Glenmuir Ltd
of Scotland for the use of their clothing range and Cotswold Golf of
Gloucester, England for their shoes.

PHOTOGRAPHIC ACKNOWLEDGEMENTS

The photographs on page 117 were supplied courtesy of
Mizuno (UK) Ltd, those on pages 119 & 120 by Titleist and Footjoy
Worldwide and Acushnet Ltd. The photograph on pages 124 and
125 was supplied by Aldila.

All the remaining photographs were taken
by Keith Hailey at East Sussex National Golf Club near Uckfield,
England one of the finest golf facilities in the world.

Library of Congress Cataloging-In-Publication
Data Available

10 9 8 7 6 5 4 3 2

Palmer, Mike.
        Systematic golf: a complete golf instruction
course/Mike Palmer.
        p.   cm.
        Includes index.
        ISBN 0-8069-0329-5
        1. Golf.   I. Title
GV965.P38   1993   92-38184
796.352—dc20   CIP

Published 1993 by Sterling Publishing Company, Inc.
387 Park Avenue South, New York, NY. 10016
First published in Great Britain by Hamlyn
an imprint of Reed Consumer Books Limited

Distributed in Canada by Sterling Publishing
c/o Canadian Manda Group, P.O. Box 920, Station U
Toronto, Ontario, Canada M8Z 5P9

Printed and bound in Singapore

ISBN 0-8069-0329-5

Contents

Introduction

THE EMERGENCE of the game of golf as one of the most popular participant sports comes as no surprise to those who have experienced even moderate success at such a rewarding leisure time pursuit.

Systematic Golf is a step by step learning programme designed to simplify the swing technique and develop a positive approach to shotmaking and playing on the golf course. It is an orderly way to develop your golfing skills, where one stage of learning logically progresses to the next. This is most clearly seen at two stages. Firstly, the newcomer to golf is encouraged to make half length swings until control and repetition are achieved before extending it to what we recognise as the complete swing. This will enable you to progress more quickly than attempting the full swing from day one. Secondly, the short game is most logically aligned such that putting is developed before chipping, pitching and finally, bunker shots. Start with the very small swings and build up.

This book is specifically suitable for golfers who are starting out playing this most fascinating game, through to established players who already have several years playing experience.

The basic fundamentals are covered in considerable depth, whilst avoiding advanced theory which only serves to complicate when simplicity should be more the objective. I hope you will conclude from this that a skilled player or professional golfer should not necessarily follow the identical set of principles to, for instance, a weekend player with an average ability. Golfers tend to fall into groups, each with a differing set of priorities and problems in improving, and swing instruction suitable for one may be most unwise for another. I instruct newcomers differently from established golfers simply because we are each individuals and the so called "perfect swing" cannot be universally applied.

Whilst everyone would be advised to adhere to the basic principles of the orthodox or model swing, it is not necessary that every swing technique should be identical. Indeed, individual preference and experimentation may lead to a mild deviation from the ideal, but so long as this strikes the ball effectively, leave it be.

Golf is an exacting game, a fact that everyone discovers at some stage. However, it need not be a difficult sport to learn if you set about improving correctly. Become knowledgeable about the basic fundamentals and make the most of the time you have available to play and practise. You can spend a lifetime studying the technical aspects of the swing and still fail to grasp the key movements to sustain gradual improvement, and many keen players fall into this trap. However, you must become more efficient in your learning if you are to progress at a rate equal to your capabilities.

If you are left handed, I offer an apology because the text and photographs will need to be converted in your mind to be of use.

I hope you enjoy reading *Systematic Golf*. To appreciate the swing and turn your knowledge into better scores on the course through constructive practise makes golf, above all else, great fun.

MIKE PALMER

The Art Of Learning Golf

Every newcomer and existing golfer has just one objective; to improve at this often frustratingly difficult game.

Consider this vital point. Most golfers who do not steadily improve as they play and practise fail because they have a poor concept of good swing technique, or the wrong idea altogether, and golf is one of those sports where the answers to problems are not always obvious, where careful swing analysis is best done by a skilled teaching professional. Even minor errors at the address position or in the swing technique affect the quality and consistency of the shots, and reduce the distance the ball flies. Golf courses and club bars are full of average players who think they know all the answers – strangely their own game never seems to show the benefit! Golf seems to breed weird and wonderful theories. The newcomer laps it all up, thirsting for the knowledge that will unlock the secrets of success.

In learning or improving the golf swing at whatever level there is just one formula which is tried and tested, and the only one worth pursuing. You have to understand exactly what you are trying to achieve as you swing the golf club, develop each position or movement until it can be enacted without conscious thought, and then practise until it is grooved into place. It amazes me how many players have little idea about what they are doing, so any success they may have is due essentially to luck.

The golf ball is just 1.68 inches (43 mm) across, the hole 4¼ inches (10.80 cm). Golf is a game of precision, in which exactness of

Left: You cannot convert a good swing concept into 'muscle-memory' without trips to the practice ground. There you can develop repetition and swing consistency by adhering to a set routine for each shot.

swing technique is a useful asset. Good golf demands a thoughtful approach and careful asessment of results. You have to plot your route around the course and play tactically positioned shots one moment, powerful and long shots the next. Golf rarely rewards the player who crashes the ball as far as possible with any old swing.

So how should you set about learning to play golf successfully? You will probably want a way to derive the most success by applying the least amount of hard work, as for most golfers practice is a chore and they would rather be on the course. I believe most players require a series of personal golf lessons by a qualified golf professional. You are trying to educate your muscle-memory, so that the correct swing movements can be repeated, semi-automatically, time after time. Standing on the tee, about to hit the ball, is NOT the moment to be thinking about all the components of a good swing. You must allow your muscle-memory to take over and concentrate your thoughts on where you want the ball to finish.

The learning process is logical enough but without a sound knowledge of swing basics you will learn slowly, if at all. Keep firmly to the fundamentals. Don't even attempt to hit a shot without a positive idea about the swing method you will need. Build up a picture in your mind about how this swing will look and how the shot will ideally be hit. Feel the movements through practice swings so that you can recall them when hitting the ball. Knowledge and understanding improve the picture of the shot and swing technique required. This in turn is translated into the 'feel' for the swing which produces the desired result. In summary:

KNOWLEDGE ➔ PICTURE ➔
FEEL ➔ SUCCESS

It is impossible to overstate the importance of starting off the swing movement correctly. There is no room for an incorrect grip as this will immediately limit improvement, and there is much to learn initially before you even consider the swing itself. However, the task is made easier by appreciating that learning is chain-reaction, and by starting from a good address position you will most easily and naturally swing the club in an orthodox manner. Take time to learn the basics and you will achieve success most easily.

The key point to stress is that if you already possess a sound understanding of the golf swing, relatively little practise will soon produce great results. The first hurdle is gathering sound knowledge. Invest in golf instruction from someone who has a trained eye plus the ability and experience to communicate what is required. You have to do your bit too. Ask yourself how good a pupil you are. Do you listen and consider each swing movement you make? Do you understand clearly and concisely what you are asked to work at? Is your mind open to fresh ideas?

Many golfers are influenced by the world-class players seen regularly on television. While they provide a tremendous inspiration to the newcomer, I would advise you to avoid trying to copy any one swing in detail. This should not prevent you from observing the good points in their swings, which can be applied when you practise and play. But note how varied the swings are, bearing in mind that each is successful in its own right. While there is no single 'perfect' swing, there has to be a swing model based purely on tried and tested fundamentals. Of course, there is room for individual variation: ultimately the only thing that matters is how well you score over 18 holes.

Pre-Swing Principles

The Address Position Routine

The type of swing you make, its basic shape and effectiveness at hitting a golf ball powerfully and accurately depend greatly on how you initially set both the club and yourself at the address position. Every successful golfer – and there are no exceptions – follows a routine in which he systematically puts the club down behind the ball and holds it there while positioning the body so that an effective swing naturally follows. Every golfer must appreciate that with these basics soundly learned, the resulting swing will most easily be achieved. If you develop bad habits at the address position you will find that your swing will forever require compensating movements to rectify the initial errors. The message is quite simple: strive to achieve the basic fundamentals at the address position, and practise them until they are fairly automatic and comfortable

The completed address position (left) combines alignment of the body with the clubface square to the target-line.

before progressing to the swing motion itself. This requires a certain discipline since every keen newcomer to the sport wants to press ahead with hitting the ball and playing the course. You may have already put your swing and game together in order to play, but don't let this prevent you from continually reviewing the basics at the address position.

Try to adhere strictly to one overall concept. You are working to learn several basic principles in a logical order and to practise them until each is easily repeatable – until muscle-memory takes over and they no longer require conscious thought to recall them.

Before examining each part of the address position, understand your ultimate objectives, or exactly why so much attention and effort should be devoted to this aspect of technique. The address position serves to target the shot correctly, so emphasis is placed on initially aiming the clubface squarely and aligning the body parallel to the

ball-to-target-line. Secondly, direction is a key factor with every shot that you hit, mostly predetermined before you even consider the swing itself. Learn to hold the club in such a way that the clubface automatically returns squarely at impact and speed can be transmitted to the clubhead. Thirdly, the address position must incorporate balance and stability so that the swing which follows will be comfortable. Lastly, you must provide an active starting position for the swing motion, keeping muscle tension light and permitting a swing with the necessary freedom to it.

It is the beginner who has the best opportunity to learn the basics correctly, with no bad habits to undo and no poor swing concepts to eradicate. If you are starting to learn golf, spend time checking and rechecking the address position until the basics are sound. Remember that a reliable and repeatable swing is most easily achieved if the address position is fundamentally correct.

Clubface Aim

Every golf shot you ever hit on the course combines direction and distance to produce the desired result. Distance is primarily a product of clubhead speed at impact; direction is basically predetermined by the address position. If you are to even begin to succeed to hit a golf ball with some accuracy, you must strive to position the clubface squarely before considering how to hold the club, stand and swing. Every shot you hit in practice

should be aimed at a target which represents the flag or center of the fairway on the golf course. Never hit shots carelessly, with no concern for directional control.

A good swing begins with the correct aim of the clubface, which must be square to an imaginary line drawn between the ball and your objective, hereafter called the *ball-to-target-line*. Aim the clubface squarely and the remainder of the correct address position is most

easily achieved. Fail at one of the most fundamental stages and you will forever have to find swing compensations in order to hit the ball straight, movements which will ensure you never play golf to your full potential.

Place the bottom 'leading-edge' of the clubface at 90 degrees to the ball-to-target-line, with the sole of the club basically flat on the ground. The club shaft should be vertical or near vertical when viewed from the front. You may angle the shaft forward very slightly towards the target, but not such that the hands are well ahead of the ball. When learning this square clubface, remember that it will need to be checked periodically, ideally by placing another club shaft down alongside the ball and parallel to the ball-to-target-line. Learn to recognize exactly how the clubface will look to you, bearing in mind that it is often deceptive when viewed from the golfer's position above and to the side of the ball. (The rules of golf forbid the use of another club shaft alongside the ball to assist with aiming in competitive play.)

The more established golfer should approach every shot in the same way, building a routine which becomes automatic when out on the course. Start by standing behind the ball, looking down the ball-to-target-line and visualizing the shot which you will need to play. You could identify a point on that line, perhaps a yard (1 m) in front of the ball, over which it should start its flight. The grass might be discoloured, or there could be a speck or small leaf already there which would assist you in squaring the clubface. It is easier to aim over a spot immediately ahead rather than having to rotate your head and look at a target in the distance.

Place the clubhead behind the ball by holding with the right hand only initially. Use another club shaft on the ground to indicate the ball-to-target-line and assist with aim and alignment when on the practice ground.

CHECKPOINTS

❍ Good aim and eventual body alignment rely on first establishing an imaginary ball-to-target-line.

❍ The bottom leading edge of the clubface must be placed down squarely to this line.

❍ Learn to recognize how a square clubface looks from above, bearing in mind it is usually somewhat deceptive.

❍ Keep the shaft vertical or tilted forward only slightly when viewed from the front.

❍ Start every address position from behind the ball, looking down the line and visualizing the shot. Pick out a spot just ahead over which the ball should fly on its way to the target.

Grip

Before even considering how the hands should be positioned on the club, I must stress the importance of the correct grip pressure. Place your no.6 iron on your little finger and find its balance point. A golf club is a relatively light object, as you can judge for yourself. It requires your hands to be placed on it, matching your overall grip pressure to the mass of the club. One of the commonest errors of many existing golfers who clearly struggle with the game is their excessive grip pressure; they hold the club so tightly that they will never achieve the necessary combination of clubface control and clubhead speed, the two most vital aspects of successful golf.

Although the terminology is to 'grip', what I really mean is that you should hold the club. Pressure must be light enough to feel exactly where the clubface is in the swing, and feel is heightened when the ends of the fingers are actually doing the holding of the club, in much the same way as a violinist holds a bow or a badminton player moves the racquet. Control is transmitted to the clubhead via your hands, but for this to be effective the wrists and lower arms must also be set at the correct level of tension. One exercise the newcomer should use, once the hands are positioned correctly on the club, is to write numbers or letters of the alphabet in the air, thus practising your correct grip pressure with its resulting freedom

extending to the wrists and lower arms. Because a golf ball has to be propelled some considerable distance it is very difficult for most new golfers to appreciate this vital aspect of the set-up. However, muscle power has relatively little to contribute to this. In reality, exactly the opposite applies. The wrists, the lower arms and hands must collectively transmit power from the larger muscles in the

back and shoulders to the clubhead within a freewheeling action. This swing will require a LIGHT grip pressure.

The Left Hand

You must be quite specific about learning the correct grip until it becomes instinctive. Take great care to position each hand on the

Open your left hand out so that the fingers point at your feet, keeping them together. Hold the very butt end of the club with your right thumb and index finger to stabilize the clubhead and prevent it from turning.

club, and check every stage. Start with the left hand position. Hold the very top end of the club between your thumb and index finger to steady it with the clubface square. You will have to adopt a basic posture even at this stage, although the checking of the posture in more detail is covered later. Push your backside out, angling the upper body forward while bending from the hips, and sit slightly through the knees. You cannot consider the grip until the body pos-

Still holding the butt end of the club, close the left hand around. It is important to have formed roughly your normal posture, tilting the upper body forward while sitting just slightly through the knees.

ture is more or less formed as the arms must hang freely downwards from the shoulders, an impossibility if the back is too upright.

Always start with the clubface actually behind the ball, and not held in the air in front of you, as some better golfers might prefer.

This way you should be more precise about keeping that clubface square to the ball-to-target-line. With your left arm hanging quite naturally from the shoulder, open the hand out and set the club diagonally across the palm and the fingers. Keep the fingers neatly together and pointing initially down towards your toe line. The club will be resting against the middle joint of the index finger and palm of the hand just above the little finger. Before folding the hand around the club, ensure you are at least half an inch (1 cm) away from the end of the club. Simply close the left hand over the club and remember to keep the grip pressure light. You will perhaps notice the fingertips holding fractionally firmer, ensuring that you are providing enough pressure to control the club, but don't hold tightly here, advice which is often incorrectly given. The correct position of the left hand will create a short thumb, barely extending lower than the crooked index finger, similar to the grip you would use for a small, light hammer. The thumb is seen to stitch itself to the index finger, keeping the position of the hand compact. The completed left hand grip will feel as though both the palm and fingers are together holding the club.

You must find a neutral position when the grip is complete. That is when both hands combine to return the clubface squarely for impact with out you having to guide or steer it. The left thumb will be just to the right of center on the club, and if a line were drawn through the center, it would point to about 11.30 on a clock face. The thumb should positively not point directly down the shaft as many club golfers tend to think. Only the fleshy part of the thumb is exactly on top, the remainder is angled more to the player's right. The next checkpoint is to count the knuckles in view from the front, seen in a mirror to check or by raising the clubhead at least 3 feet (1 m) in the air to look down on your hand. Keep the toe end of the clubhead in the air as you do

this and your eyes positioned centrally, rather than inclined to your left as is the tendency. Look for two whole knuckles and a small part of the third. If a fourth is in view, the hand must be rotated a touch to your left on the club.

Left Hand Grip Errors

It will take time and some practice to ensure your left hand is consistently placed correctly on the club and to feel comfortable in that position. Many golfers fall into basic errors at this early stage that affect how they play quite dramatically. Serious swing problems often originate from a faulty grip. The worst position for the left hand is to the left of neutral, holding the club too much in the fingers and

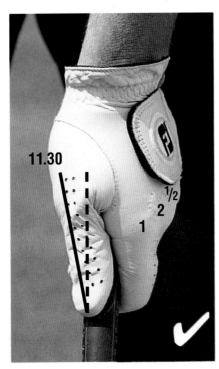

✔ CORRECT ✔
An orthodox left hand position showing two and a half knuckles when viewed from the front. The thumb is fractionally to the player's right of center.

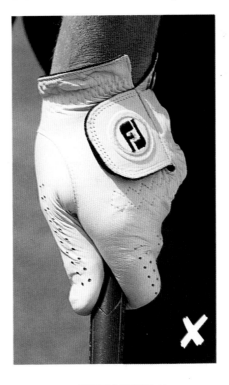

✘ INCORRECT ✘
If the left hand is positioned too far to the player's right, three and a half or four knuckles are in view. Although the preferred term is 'right of neutral' most people refer to this grip as 'strong'.

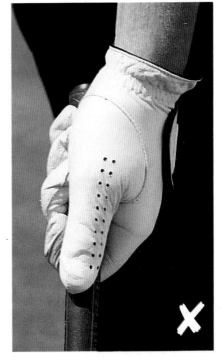

✘ INCORRECT ✘
Although the end of the thumb is correctly positioned, the remainder of the hand is positioned 'weakly' or to the left of neutral. This will inhibit clubhead speed as well as tending to return the clubface 'open' at impact.

✔ CORRECT ✔
The ideal position of the left hand will keep the fingers neatly together as the thumb barely extends beneath the index finger. This compact grip will maximize control and still permit the wrists to hinge freely in the swing.

✔ CORRECT ✔
From this angle, the left hand can clearly be seen to be holding away from the end, with the club sitting comfortably across the palm and fingers.

✗ INCORRECT ✗
A long left thumb extended down the club is an indication that the palm of the hand has no control over the club, and when the hand is opened out, this club will be seen to be incorrectly held more across the fingers.

MODERN GRIP TERMINOLOGY

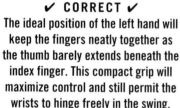

In order to remain consistent with golfing terminology, I have used the term 'strong' to describe a grip where one or both of the hands are positioned to the player's right of neutral. While this grip positively FEELS stronger and more powerful, it is an unfortunate description which often leads golfers to hold on more tightly. As you should have concluded from the section about the grip, a LIGHT pressure is most advantageous, assisting you in making a free-wheeling swing action to generate clubhead speed. It would be far better to describe this 'strong' grip as 'right of neutral'.

You will recall that neutral describes the optimum positioning of your hands - a major contributory factor to the clubface automatically returning squarely for impact. For the vast majority of golfers, this will be based on two and a half knuckles being in view on the left hand, and the right hand covering the left thumb but still showing the ends of the fingers when viewed from the front.

The 'weak' position of the hands describes where one or more is positioned too far to the player's left on the club and although it unquestionably FEELS weak, it is better described as left of neutral.

creating a fist. The club will certainly not sit in the crooked forefinger, and the wrist will be turned out, resulting in very weak and inaccurate shots, generally to the right of target. While the pad is correctly positioned, the remainder of the thumb is too far left, the palm of the hand never really holding the club enough to control it. As the player looks down to check the position, only one full knuckle is in view.

Remember that the hand must find neutral, showing two and a half knuckles from the player's viewpoint when raising the clubhead from the ground. If the hand is to the left of neutral, it is said to be 'weakly' positioned, although this has nothing to do with grip pressure. If the club is being held

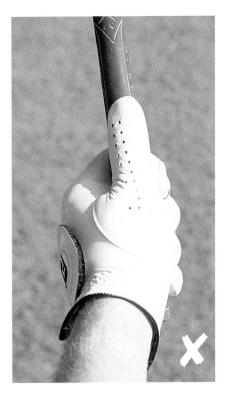

✔ CORRECT ✔
As the club is lifted up in front of you, look for the thumb pointing a touch to the left, and from this position you should be able to count the knuckles to confirm if your left hand is correct. Notice also that the thumb is 'stitched' to the index finger.

✗ INCORRECT ✗
If the thumb points to the right side then the grip may be left of neutral or too 'weakly' positioned on the club. Barely one knuckle is in view from this angle, instead of the more usual two and a half.

✗ INCORRECT ✗
Not only is the left hand too far to the right on the club or too 'strongly' positioned, the left thumb has separated from the index finger.

correctly in the combination of palm plus fingers, but the hand is turned to the players left, the clubface is unlikely to return squarely on impact. This faulty grip will show less than two and a half knuckles. The opposite to this and certainly the less troublesome of these errors is when the hand is placed too much to the player's right on the club, showing more than two and a half knuckles. This 'strong' position is most likely to return the clubface to the left of target at impact, hitting the ball with a curve in that direction. To the golfer, this faulty position often feels exactly how it's described, strong and therefore powerful. This makes it difficult to change if used for any length of time, so check the knuckles periodically to avoid slipping into these most basic errors.

Adding The Right Hand

Always remember that the hands will eventually form one unit on the club. They must work together; they combine to provide control and power. I will start by explaining the overlapping grip, sometimes referred to as the Vardon grip. It is the choice of most of the top class golfers the world over and should be the starting point for everyone with only the odd exception, of which more later. Basically, the palm of the right hand must face the target, and the hold is much more in the fingers than with the left hand. The beginner is espe-

cially conscious of the difference in the feel of each hand, the left combining the palm and fingers to really hold the club, while the right hand must control the clubface, the initial feeling being that you are only gripping with your fingertips. This is not strictly true, but keep it in mind as you learn the correct position.

The direction the palm faces is critical to clubface control in the swing, and this forms the basis of how the hand is placed on the club. Start by forming the correct spread of the hand, opening a gap at the little finger and forefinger, the middle two staying together. If your fingers are not supple it will take some practice, but this spread of the hand will influence how successful the completed grip will

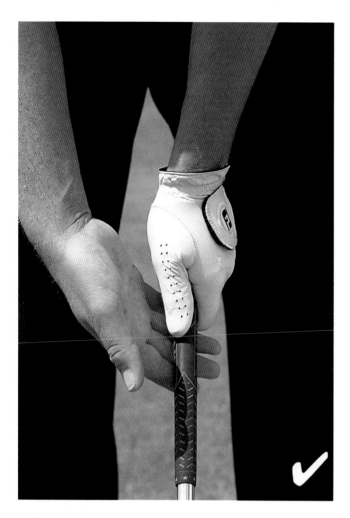

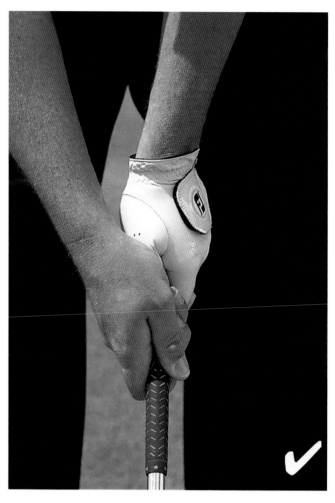

✔ CORRECT ✔
The initial stage of the right hand grip overlaps the little finger and then closes the two middle fingers around the club. Note that the middle joints of the fingers are holding the club in order that the right palm will face the target in the completed grip.

✔ CORRECT ✔
The completed grip shows how the right hand has closed over to conceal the left thumb. The lowest point of the right hand is the index finger, keeping the right thumb in a compact position, not stretched down.

be. Overlap the little finger of the right hand over the lower two of the left. Let the finger sit on top and don't force it to wrap around or the palm of the hand will be pulled underneath, losing the prime objective of the palm facing the target. Add the two middle fingers on to the club, butting them up to touch the index finger of the left, the club being held most positively in the end two joints of both fingers. Keep the forefinger separated, and fold it

around in a trigger position, always staying slightly away from the others. This sets the hand in a position to both control the clubface and provide the necessary leverage in the swing motion. It will ultimately provide power to the shots. Lastly, the thumb flattens onto the club, but with only the fleshy part touching the rubber grip. The remainder covers the left thumb, hiding it from view completely when viewed from above.

The right hand should be compactly positioned on the club, again keeping the thumb short, the lowest point being the triggered finger. The thumb must follow the similar direction to the left, angled towards the 11 o'clock or 11.30 position, but not straight downwards. The fleshy part of the thumb should lie to the player's

left on the club, but not so far over that the ends of the middle fingers are hidden from view.

Right Hand Grip Errors

Since golf demands control over direction and the right hand most influences this, existing golfers who habitually hit shots to the right or left of the target should first review their grip. I must stress that the correct right hand position comes slowly to

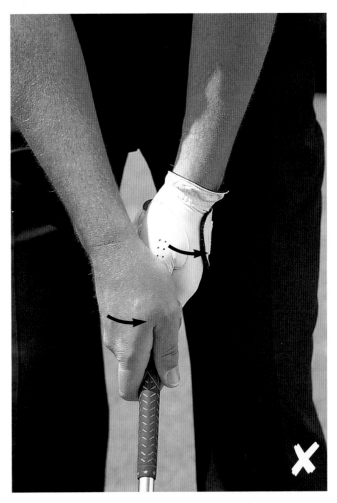

Neither hand is correctly positioned, but at least they can work together as one unit as BOTH are turned to the player's right. More than two and a half knuckles are in view on the left and the palm of the right hand doesn't face the target.

many beginners, often with initial discomfort, and I therefore see many basic errors at this stage. The most common mistake is to position the right hand too 'strongly' on the club, the palm of the hand moving more underneath the club, palm facing upwards instead of at the target. The thumb will invariably follow, moving to the right of center, usually stretching the thumb down the club and losing the effect of control through the combination of thumb and triggered index finger. This same error can be pro-

duced by the small finger of the right hand wrapping excessively around the left, protruding from behind the knuckles of the left and placing the club too much in the palm of the hand. This 'strong' right hand position will feel very powerful, as the grip is moved away from the fingers and more into the palm of the hand, but as it reverts to its most natural position for impact the clubface will turn left, curving the ball in that direction. Once badly learned, this is also one of the most awkward areas of the grip to change, the necessary alteration of moving the hand to the player's left initially feeling very weak. The less frequently seen error is when the right hand sits too far left on the club, a 'weak' position which covers the ends of the middle fingers of the left hand.

The hands can work as one unit together but they are both too far to the player's left, showing just one knuckle on the left and the palm of the right hand doesn't face the target. At impact both hands tend to revert to neutral as the clubface returns 'open'.

The palm of the right hand will be directed more downwards and the clubface will tend to return facing to the right at impact as both hands try to find their more natural positions.

Practising The Grip

Every golf shot you will ever hit in practice or on the course will be a separate event, with a new grip formed each and every time. Don't

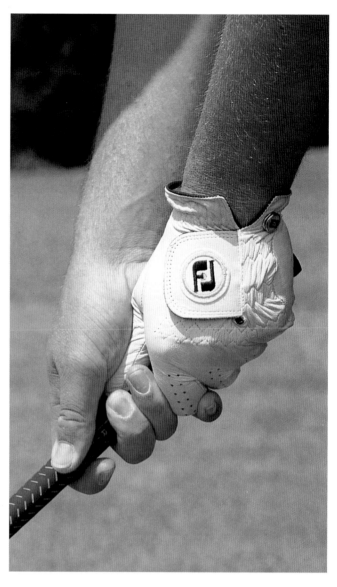

The right hand is added by overlapping the small finger before the two middle fingers close around, keeping them together all the time. Notice how the fingers of the right hand principally hold the club, not the palm of the hand.

When the right hand grip is completed, you should notice a gap between the index finger and the middle two fingers. The index finger and thumb add to control in the completed swing. The hands are now one compact unit which can work together in the swing.

fall into the habit of retaining your grip while moving another practice ball into place. After one shot, break the grip and start afresh, in exactly the same way as you will later on the golf course.

Buy yourself a leather or synthethic golf glove, worn only on the left hand to provide a better contact with the club. The thin material will hardly prevent blisters if you practise more than your skin can stand. Keep the glove in its original wrapping to help it retain moisture and serve you better, and buy one which is quite snug fitting initially as they stretch in use in order to fit your hand. The principal importance of using a left hand glove from day one is to make sure that you hold the club securely without excessive grip pressure.

Most golfers find learning the correct grip quite difficult. Some never succeed with this most basic part of playing the game properly, and it's no wonder they never attain the level of ability they are capable of achieving. Accept that the grip may feel most awkward and uncomfortable initially but by constantly checking and re-checking, you can learn to automatically position your hands correctly every time. Such repetitiveness will take practice by holding a club whenever you have a few moments spare, indoors or out. A golf professional can make you a grip end for you to

The right hand is added by overlapping the small finger, keeping the middle two fingers neatly together and folding them around the club. Notice that the palm of the right hand hasn't yet touched the grip, the fingers being the only contact at this stage.

practice while sitting down at home, familiarizing yourself with the correct hand positions until you can quickly and easily find the same place every time. Develop the sequence described earlier. Hold the very end of the club in the right hand, add the left, then the right. One, two, three, completed quickly and without needing to check every time. Try to avoid any fidgeting with the hands once in place, as this may lead to them creeping into incorrect positions.

The completed grip will keep the fingers of the right hand separated with the exception of the middle two. The club sits across the middle joint of the right index finger and the thumb holds it in place, maximizing control.

✗ INCORRECT ✗
The left hand is at neutral, but the right hand is too far over to the player's left. Although unusual, this error will lead to an 'open' clubface at impact as the right hand reverts to its more natural position.

✗ INCORRECT ✗
The left hand is at neutral, but the right is incorrectly positioned, the palm certainly not facing the target. This 'strong' right hand grip will tend to revert to neutral at impact, 'closing' the clubface.

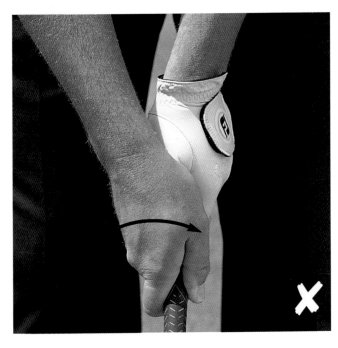

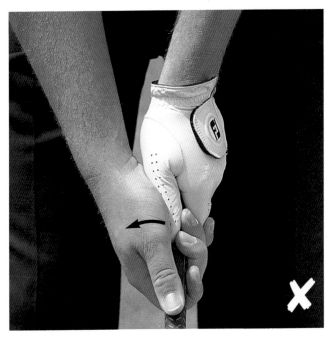

Left: You should raise your arms into the air, lifting the clubhead to view your grip position. When doing this, keep the angle formed between the arms and shaft of the club. An alternative to this would be to look in a mirror to check.

Overlapping, Interlocking And Baseball Grips

The exact function of the completed grip is easy enough to understand. The hands must firstly be positioned on the club so that you achieve clubface control, influencing the direction of the ball's flight. Secondly, the hands must work together to provide control and transmit power, hence the overlap of the small finger of the right and compactness of both hands. Thirdly, the grip pressure established must be light enough to permit a free swinging action through impact and beyond, an essential ingredient in developing clubhead speed. The overlapping grip is the obvious choice for most golfers. This type of grip will serve you well initially, and it will require only minor adjustments, if any, as your golfing ability increases.

There are two alternative types of grip, each one a relatively small variation from the overlapping grip. The more widely used alter-native is the interlocking grip, used successfully by a few professional golfers, particularly those who find it very difficult to separate the fingers on the right hand, usually because the hands are small or the fingers short. The left hand is established in the usual way, but before placing the right hand on the club, raise the index finger of the left off the club and cross it with the small finger of the right. The middle two fingers and thumb follow in the normal way. It is essential that the fundamental positioning of the hands

The overlapping grip is preferred by most golfers and should be the choice of any newcomer to the sport with just the odd exception. The small finger of the right hand overlaps the index finger of the left to keep the hands as one unit.

CHECKPOINTS

○ The club should lie across the palm and fingers of your left hand, and when the hand is closed around the thumb will 'stitch' itself to the index finger.

○ Two and a half knuckles will be seen if the club is raised into the air, or by looking into a mirror ahead.

○ An overlapping grip folds the small finger of the right hand over the left, the middle two fingers are together on the rubber grip and the index finger forms a trigger.

○ Practise right hand separation, holding your two middle fingers together while forming gaps with the others.

○ The right palm must remain facing the target after it has folded around the club to provide directional control.

○ The grip pressure should remain constantly light at the address position, resisting any tendency to squeeze the club.

○ Stick with the correct grip position until it becomes more comfortable after some practice. A faulty grip will do nothing for your game.

○ Invest in a quality leather golf glove, worn on your left hand to assist with contacting the club more positively without relying on increased grip pressure.

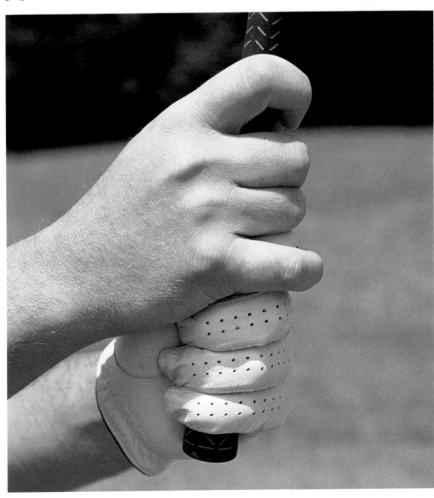

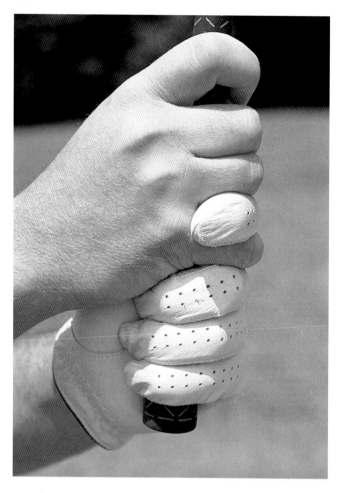 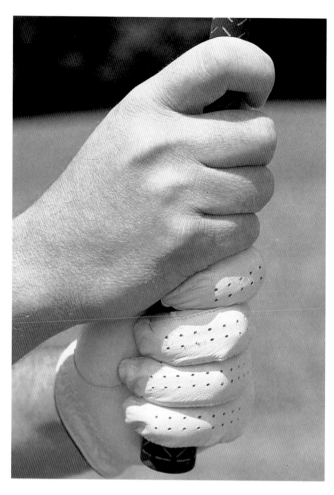

The interlocking grip still unifies the hands but many golfers find this alternative uncomfortable. The placement of the hands remains identical to the overlapping grip, but the more secure feeling that this grip can offer is preferred by some.

The 'baseball grip' involves no overlap or interlock but must still keep the hands working as one unit. It is essential that the upper three fingers of the right hand are neatly together, and butted up against the index finger of the left.

remains the same as with the overlapping grip, and you should be able to interchange from one to the other without moving the basic position of either hand. Some golfers find this interlock position more comfortable, and that is as good enough a reason to use it as any, but I certainly see more errors resulting from an interlocking grip than an overlapping one. The usual difficulty is the exact placement of the right hand, the interlocking golfer often jamming his fingers deeply together, the right hand never finding its position with the palm facing the target. This faulty position holds the club excessively in the palm and first finger joints, the palm faces upwards too much and the thumb usually falls to the right of center. The hand is placed too 'strongly' on the club, which will lead to a closed clubface at impact. The golfer who chooses the interlocking grip must pay particular attention to the right hand, especially how the small finger rests against the left index finger.

The second variation is the baseball grip, often used by golfers with small hands and children or senior golfers who require more leverage through separating the wrists a touch more. This is positively not a grip for a skilled golfer, and has to be amended in the case of juniors if they are to ever control the flight of the golf ball as their hands become stronger. The advantages of this grip are obvious, being simple enough to learn, requiring less attention to the correct hand separation, and enjoying the added benefit of transmitting more power to the ball through added leverage. However, the hands are generally too far apart with this type of grip as playing ability progresses, as stronger hands less compactly placed on the club tend to oppose one another, affecting clubface control and most likely hitting the ball all over the course. For the young golfer prepared to upgrade to the overlapping grip later, this variation is worth trying.

Golf Ball Placement

The address position involves setting yourself in the very best place from which to swing effectively. The clubface provides the contact with the ball, determining its flight and direction, but ultimately YOU provide the necessary clubhead speed. Stand correctly, the right distance from the ball with it positioned opposite the feet and you can make a most simple, but effective swing. If the clubhead is to meet the back of the golf ball every time solidly and squarely, the body must be positioned such that you can swing freely through impact, never needing to adjust or guide the club. The newcomer to golf should realize that if these basics are established, it becomes easier to swing well.

Start by learning how far to stand from the ball, an aspect of the address position that is best learned in conjunction with good posture, as one creates the other to a large extent. Start with your feet together, directly opposite the golf ball. Remember to keep the upper body angled forward, bending at the hips and keeping the chin up. Slightly flex the knees, and let the arms hang naturally from the shoulders. This will tell you how far to stand from the ball, as the comfort of this position will dictate that the wrists must retain a slight angle, formed between the arms and club shaft. You have only one distance to learn initially, keeping it as simple to learn as possible. Once you have established one distance correctly, it is relatively easy

Start with your feet together before stepping off the stance. Ensure the ball is located centrally to the feet by checking in a mirror.

Step the left foot out 4 inches (10 cm) at the heel, angling the toe out some 20 degrees at the same time. Every standard golf shot with a full swing will require this same initial move to correctly position the ball in the stance.

to adjust for longer and shorter shaft lengths after the basic swing is learned. With your no.6 iron, the hands will be some 8 inches (20 cm) from the left thigh, just above the knee, but it is not essential that this is measured or strictly adhered to as we are each different

The right foot is opened out 8 inches (20 cm) at the heel, again angling the toe out about 20 degrees for maximum stability. This is a no.6 iron and the completed stance is about a shoulders width.

✗ INCORRECT ✗
A very common error of positioning the golf ball too far to the player's left, excessively forward in the stance. Not only is the ball most unlikely to be at the base of the swing arc, but the upper body tends to respond by aligning the shoulders left of target, so compounding problems.

in build, and the comfort of your natural distance is more beneficial. I would avoid one habit which many beginners try, dropping the end of the club onto the left leg to measure off the distance from the ball. This changes everything you have previously positioned

✗ INCORRECT ✗
Less commonly seen, the ball is positioned too far back in the stance. The upper body tends to align to the right of target as a result, and the clubhead is likely to be still descending as contact is made.

✗ INCORRECT ✗

A poor address position due to the ball being too close to the player's feet, causing the back to be a touch too upright and the hands too close to the left thigh. There will not be enough space for the arms and club to swing freely through impact.

CHECKPOINTS

○ Golf ball placement combines the distance from the ball with the position in the stance relative to the feet.

○ Having formed a basic posture, check that there is a gap of some 8 inches (20 cm) between your left thigh and the back of your left hand with a mid iron.

○ If you are the correct distance from the ball, your upper arms will very lightly brush your chest.

○ Begin to learn the ball position by starting with your feet together and open the left out some 4 inches (10 cm) and your right twice that amount.

○ Turn your toes out 20 degrees for maximum stability.

○ Learn to recognize the correct position of the ball visually, remembering that it is usually deceptive.

✗ INCORRECT ✗

This very bad address position is often the result of trying to keep the head down and, in addition, the ball is positioned too far away from the player. As a result of this the back is angled excessively forward and the body will be rather out of balance during the swing.

correctly, especially the basic posture, and really is unnecessary. Trust what seems most natural and you will find it most comfortable, since distance from the ball is learned through feel, not by measuring. Sense that the insides of the upper arms very lightly brush the sides of your chest, one checkpoint which will certainly prevent the common error of reaching excessively for the ball.

Once the distance from the ball is established, you must then focus on the position of the ball, making sure that it is in front of your eyes, not too far towards the target, or too far back towards the right foot.

Start with the ball located central to the two feet placed together. Step the left foot out some 4 inches (10 cm) at the heel, turning the toe outwards approximately 20 degrees. Open the right foot out some 8 inches (20 cm) again angling the toe out. You must ensure that your weight is evenly distributed between left and right, and likewise from toes to heels. This is necessary in a golf swing which demands balance and stability if it is ever to be powerful and under control. Above all, you should strive to recognize how the correct position looks from over the ball, and remember that it is often deceptive.

Body Alignment

Logic will tell you that if you want to hit the golf ball straight, you have to both aim the clubface squarely and then align the whole body in that direction too. The usual analogy given by teaching professionals is the body aligns itself on one side of a railway track, while the ball sits on the other rail, the two lines being parallel, of course. In reality, it is very difficult to align the body consistently square, facing the ball and with the shoulders, hips, knees and toes all parallel to the ball-to-target-line. The novice usually experiences two problems. If you are a natural sportsperson, the fact that you have to face at 90 degrees away from the target will feel most

unusual; most ball sports are played facing or half facing the bowler or opponent. Secondly, the right shoulder must sit lower than the left at the address position, a fact which is obvious when you consider the right hand is set at a lower level on the club, but takes some getting used to. The beginner often finds the tilted shoulder line unnatural and in an attempt to

✔ CORRECT ✔

Good alignment generally follows good aim of the clubface, squarely to the ball-to-target-line. The toes, knees, hips and shoulders should all be parallel to the target-line in the completed address position. From here, you are most likely to hit consistently straight shots.

level the body, the right shoulder can move forward and towards the golf ball, misaligning the shoulders to the left of target. Rarely will the beginner align the shoulders to the right of target, unless there is an over emphasis placed on the lower right shoulder.

The objective is to align the whole body squarely to the ball-to-target-line, so ask a friend to position a club shaft across the body, especially the shoulders, to confirm that you are actually in the correct position. Once set-up, the feeling is that if you rotate the head towards the target you sense the left shoulder in view far more noticeably than the right shoulder if you turn your head to the right. It is actually possible to check your own alignment by holding the club in its normal position, then keeping quite still with the upper body while moving the shaft across your shoulder line, holding

CHECKPOINTS

❍ While the clubface will obviously point at the target, the shoulders, hips, knees and toes will seem to be aligned to the left of target.

❍ Be aware of the fact that the right shoulder will be lower than the left, often feeling as though the shoulders are aligned to the right.

❍ The emphasis must be on the shoulders being square, and if so the hips and feet will tend to follow automatically.

❍ The shoulders are the key to good alignment, so ask a friend to check with another shaft laid across them.

❍ As you rotate your head to view the target as a final check, feel as though you are looking over your left shoulder a touch.

✗ INCORRECT ✗

Left: The shoulders are left of target, pulling the hips, knees and toes round that way too. From this faulty address position the swing must find a compensation to hit the ball at the target, adding complications which should be avoided.

✗ INCORRECT ✗

Right: The shoulders, hips, knees and toes are clearly aligned to the right of target, usually because the clubface is aimed incorrectly to the right to begin with. Hitting the shot at the target from such a poor alignment will be very difficult, and will cause further swing errors in attempting to do so.

with just your right hand. After a while you will find the correct position over and again without needing to concentrate on it. With

practice, it will become instinctive, will begin to look right and above all, will feel very comfortable.

Your body alignment, will prin-

cipally dictate the overall shape to your completed swing, its plane, width and effectiveness at striking the ball.

Body Posture

By following each stage of the pre-swing principles you will have already set a basic body posture. This is necessary even before you learn to hold the golf club in order to position the hands correctly, the arms hanging naturally from the shoulders, the upper body position dependent upon the backside being pushed out and the knees flexed a little. We now check this posture prior to learning the swing motion.

If the swing is to be easily learned and its movements kept as

✗ INCORRECT ✗

A poor posture, but easily remedied by the player simply pushing his bottom out more and letting his arms hang more freely downwards from the shoulders. Here, the wrists are pushed upwards which will not assist them in correctly hingeing later in the swing.

simple as possible while still ensuring they are effective, the correct body posture, pre-set at the address position, plays a vital role. The fully assembled swing moves around the spine angle. The shoulders will turn at 90 degrees to the spine and therefore if the angle is not correct at the address position, one or more adjustments will have to be made mid-swing, movements which will lead to mis-hit shots and inconsistency. The importance of the body posture is generally underestimated, perhaps explaining why so many bad golfers fail at this vital point.

The basics are easy enough to follow. Angle the spine forward, the bend coming from the hips, not the waist. Keep the chin high, away from the chest, and at this point I would stress that you do not need to keep you head down to play golf

✗ INCORRECT ✗

A perfectly good posture with the obvious exception of the upper spine angle. The head is far too low, and is certain to restrict the freedom required for a good shoulder turn in the backswing. However bad this looks, so many golfers start their swings off from here because they have incorrectly been told to keep their head down.

✗ INCORRECT ✗

If this player were to simply sit through the knees, the address position would be fine. However, with the legs locked back in this way it looks very uncomfortable, tense in the muscles and is certainly not an address position from which a well-balanced and successful swing can be made.

CHECKPOINTS

○ If you are to hit effective shots, your body posture is important and will influence the overall shape of the swing.

○ The spine angle is set by tilting forward from the hips while sitting just slightly through the knees.

○ Your head must sit up on top of your shoulders and not be buried in your chest.

○ Your arms must hang downwards from your shoulders and form an angle at the shaft of the club.

○ The ideal posture will evenly distribute weight between toes and heels.

successfully. The reverse is more applicable, as good posture involves the head sitting up on the shoulders, your eyes having to look down a little to fully view the golf ball. Feel that your upper chest is actually facing forward, not down at the ground. The higher head position will permit the shoulders to turn more freely in the swing later, but for now I would ask you to forget any advice to keep your head down. It leads many novices to bury their heads in their chest, cramping the swing movements and actually contributing to bad shotmaking. Check that your weight has remained evenly distributed between toes and heels, and evenly between the left and right side. Feel as though the small of your back is slightly concave, emphasizing further the necessity to make room to swing the golf club past the body in the completed swing. Allow the arms to hang naturally from the shoulders, their correct position being most easily achieved when the spine angle is ideal. The very worst posture you can adopt, and quite a frequent error, is to fail to bend enough from the hips, the back being too near vertical and the wrists arched over. From this position you really have no chance of striking the ball consistently, and never with good clubhead speed as the poor posture limits swing freedom.

Developing
the Basic Swing

The easiest way to progress is to start off with a mini-swing and build from there. You should learn a half-length swing first and gradually extend it until you develop the more complete action. Effectively, there are two learning stages for the beginner, starting with this mini-swing before incorporating the same action within a conventional length swing. The reasons for this are simple enough. Every existing golfer is reliant upon hand/eye co-ordination to some extent. This is your ability to see the ball in front of you and return the club-head to strike it repetitively, a skill which most sports-oriented people already possess, but which for many has to be learned at the same time as the basic fundamentals.

Left: Three-quarters into the through swing, the shaft now at horizontal and above the player's left shoulder. The hips and shoulders now fully face the target and the weight is almost entirely on the left side.

If you cannot borrow hand/eye co-ordination from tennis, squash, hockey or another similar sport you already play, you may have to develop the skill as you practise. For you, going to the full swing immediately would prove very difficult, the failures excessive, your enthusiasm and enjoyment severely knocked. Don't imagine that learning golf is a gradual progression along the learning curve to reach your objectives. There are bound to be some hiccups along the way, but if you have basics to review and a mini-swing to revert to temporarily to solve the problems, you will improve more quickly and find the bad days annoying but never totally infuriating!

Ultimately, the full swing will incorporate rhythm, a term describing how fluid the movements are. Initially, each of these movements is learned as a stationary position with various checks made at each stage. Once these are learned, the movements are linked up, into one complete action. Learn to isolate each stage described, so that you can look at each component and recognize both how it looks and feels. After a short time, muscle-memory will take over and it won't require conscious thought any longer. Be realistic about what you are able to achieve at any one time, bearing in mind the fact that a golf swing lasts just a couple of seconds. It is impossible to work at everything at the same time, human learning capacity limiting you to just one or perhaps two thoughts each swing but never more. When you are practising be prepared to take many, many practise swings, as this will be more beneficial than hitting one ball after another. You will steadily progress if you adhere to simple swing concepts Keep your thoughts positive always and think about what you should be doing, and not about a series of 'don'ts'. You will learn most effectively with a positive attitude.

The Half Swing Exercise

The completed address position routine has positioned you such that the swing can be learned most easily. At first glance it is a stationary position, but don't freeze over the shot by standing motionless over the ball. Instead, move the clubhead a little, keep the body muscles active and ready to set the swing in motion.

The first movement away from the ball which starts the backswing is dictated by a turn of the shoulders, the stomach and hips responding by also turning. The arms will naturally want to move the clubhead back on a gentle but wide arc around the body. I would encourage you to sense the right shoulder initiating the backswing turn, as most players feel this easier than pushing the left shoulder across. I must emphasize the TURN of the shoulders, the spine angle remaining constant. The path of the clubhead must almost immediately move inside a straight line drawn back from the ball, as an extension to the ball-to-target-line. Don't attempt to take the clubhead straight back, but instead allow it to follow the more elliptical path dictated by the body turn. Stop when the club has reached 8 o'clock, before the shaft is parallel to the ground. At this point the wrists and arms will be in basically the same relative positions as at the set-up. The key is to move all the swing components together to initiate the swing. The upper body turns at exactly the same time as the arms and club move back.

Continue the combination movement of the shoulders and arms until the club shaft reaches 9 o'clock, or parallel to the ground. The hands will begin to hinge a touch in this second part of the backswing, causing the right elbow to tuck in towards the right hip. The left arm remains comfortably extended throughout while the right elbow folds to accommodate the hinging of the wrists. Racquet sport players will recognize the correct feeling of the right wrist folding back on itself, a potentially powerful movement and a most influential component of the completed swing. Avoid any movement which allows the wrists to rotate independently.

Halfway into the backswing, at the completion of the mini-swing, you can easily check the following points, all of which are in view. First, the shoulders have completed a turn of some 40 degrees, the hips half that and the right knee has begun to straighten. The left knee will have moved towards the ball with an increased flex from that set at the address position. Limit the lower body movement by keeping your left heel on the

The first backswing move takes the club to 8 o'clock, and combines a shoulder turn with an armswing. At this point there is no hinge of the wrists at all, but the right elbow softens or very slightly folds. You might already sense a touch of weight shift onto the right leg.

ground, not even allowing the foot to roll. Effectively, the lower body is resisting the turning of the upper body. Check that the club shaft at nine o'clock is also parallel to the ball-to-target-line, and if you imagine a clock face around the clubhead the bottom leading

CHECKPOINTS

○ At 8 o'clock the arms have combined with an upper body turn with no conscious hinge of the wrists at all.

○ As the shaft reaches parallel to the ground in the backswing, check that the left arm is comfortably extended while the right folds away towards the hip.

○ The shaft should be parallel to the ball-to-target-line and the clubface leading edge is at 11.30 on a clock face.

○ Ensure that the shoulders are half turned to your right side at halfway back.

○ Don't stop at impact but instead continue to 4 o'clock, again resisting any tendency to use the wrists, but turning the shoulders through while swinging from the arms only.

○ As the club shaft reaches parallel to the ground, the wrists will have hinged slightly to point the toe end into the sky.

○ Encourage weight transference even in this mini-swing by shifting the right knee to the target side until raised at the heel.

edge should be at 11.30, not quite straight up but close to it.

Now simply reverse the direction of these movements slowly and gradually, moving through the starting point and on towards 4 o'clock, the club shaft stopping short of horizontal to begin with.

The club can be seen to move on a gentle arc around the body dictated by the shoulders turning around the pivot point. The right leg has already begun to straighten as the left bends a touch more.

Mirror image the equivalent position in the backswing, checking that the left shoulder has turned to partially face the target, and both arms are extended with only a light tension in the arm muscles. The club has travelled on an imaginary line gently around the body,

The swing reference point at halfway back is most important in order to check that each component of the swing is moving correctly. The shoulder turn is about 40 degrees while the hips have turned half this amount.

The shoulders can be seen to have half turned to the right while the left arm is controlling the radius to the swing. Look how the right elbow has begun to noticeably fold away towards the hip.

dictated by the turn of the upper body, so don't force the club towards the target. At this point you should sense the right heel wanting to lift. That is the only principal difference between this

and its corresponding position the other side of the swing. As you continue to move the club to 3 o'clock, or parallel to the ground level, the right heel will lift more. Even at this early stage, the inten-

tion is to develop the correct lower body action and weight transference which is part of the completed swing. At halfway through, the shoulders will have turned some 60 degrees, the hips about the same,

✗ INCORRECT ✗
In a correct backswing the elbows should remain fairly close together. In this bad halfway back position, the right elbow has been forced away from the hip as the clubface is 'closed', facing more down at the ground than it should.

the left leg will begin to straighten and the right knee will have moved across towards the left, increasing its bend in doing so. The club shaft should be on a parallel line to the ball-to-target-line, and a line drawn across the bottom leading edge of the clubface will once again point to 11.30 on an imaginary clock face. I must emphasize that the right arm is extended at this point while the left arm has folded slightly downwards and in towards the left hip.

If you have believed that the left arm must remain straight throughout the swing remember that the swing is, in simplistic terms, a mirror image each side

The hands have independently rolled early into the backswing, forcing the right elbow too close into the body as a result. The back of the left hand should be facing ahead of the player, not angled more upward as can be clearly seen here.

and the left arm must give and eventually fold after impact in basically the same way as the right must fold in the backswing. Furthermore, forget the word straight as this is often taken too literally, encouraging golfers to apply excessive tension, limiting freedom to the swing. The left arm is never purposely forced to be straight, but more 'comfortably extended' when at its full radius.

Notice that you don't stop at impact to review any position, as you always swing THROUGH impact, never to the ball. This becomes important later as we will learn to develop a free-wheeling

A NEUTRAL CLUBFACE

Since good golf relies on how successfully you control the clubface throughout the swing, you should be quite specific about the positions which have to be learned or reviewed. Although the clubface could be described as 'toe end up' at halfway into the backswing, this is technically incorrect. In fact, only a backswing which rotates the hands excessively will point the head exactly into the sky, so encouraging an independent and compensatory wrist action through impact which leads to inconsistency. The correct position will direct the bottom leading edge of the clubface at 11.30 on an imaginary clockface, thus hinging the wrists and not rolling the hands. The clock face idea is the easiest way to remember the correct position as it is difficult to describe it any other way.

Although this position could be called 'square', I much prefer the word 'neutral', in terms of it being correct relative to the degree of body turn at that point.

✔ CORRECT ✔
The player should review clubface control at halfway into the backswing by checking that a line across the leading edge will point at 11.30 on an imaginary clock face. This is a square or neutral position, and involves the wrists hingeing a touch.

✗ INCORRECT ✗
The back of the left hand should face ahead, but is seen here to be directed more at the ground. The clubface is 'closed', and a line drawn across the leading edge points more at 10 o'clock. This error is generally associated with shots which curve left.

✗ INCORRECT ✗
This backswing has rolled the hands excessively early on, and a line drawn across the leading edge would be directed at about 12.30. This is associated with shots which curve to the right. Although not a common error, clubface control from here onwards will be difficult to recover.

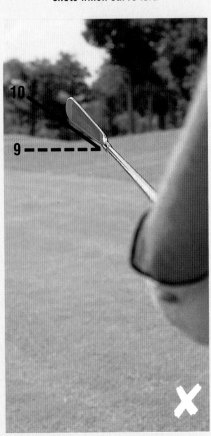

Left and below: The shaft is now at the 4 o'clock position, and shows how the upper body has moved around its pivot point between the shoulders, resisting any tendency to hinge at the wrists. Notice also that the right side has moved the weight over, the heel having left the ground. This is basically a mirror image of its corresponding position the other side of the swing, with the exception of the right knee and foot.

action which doesn't involve a hit impulse. You don't HIT a golf ball as such, but, rather, swing through impact to sweep the ball away. You may be aware of the sensation of the right hand action, folding at the wrist in the backswing and ROTATING over the left hand through the hitting area. Take plenty of practice swings until you are familiar enough with the swing to simply blend each stage together.

Left: An ideal position at halfway through, or 3 o'clock. The shoulders are half turned towards the target, the weight is clearly on the left side and the right arm is fully extended to maintain swing radius. The left arm has 'given' a touch or slightly folded inwards and downwards.

✔ **CORRECT** ✔

Below: From this angle, a line across the bottom edge of the clubface can be seen to point at 11.30 on a clock as the player sees it. The shoulders and hips have both more than half turned towards the target and the weight is mostly on the targetside leg, the right foot at least half raised.

Focus your eyes on the ground and learn to brush the grass away as the club swings through. Keep the backswing smooth and easy, but gently accelerate in the downswing to begin to encourage a change in pace which is part of every good player's rhythm and tempo. Finally, you can introduce the golf ball. Beginners should play their first shots off tee-pegs to build confidence. Accept that some shots will

Left: An incorrect position at halfway through. The left arm has continued too straight and has pulled the upper body around too soon. The shoulders and hips at this point should be turning to face the target, but not as much as shown here.

✗ INCORRECT ✗

Below: The effect of locking the left arm up too long into the forward swing is to inhibit the correct hinging of the wrists. The clubface has been left 'open', and a line running across the leading edge will point at roughly 1 o'clock.

be less than ideal, but most will travel 60 yards or so towards the target. Your initial success is down to how thoroughly you have learned these basics and how well you are able to apply them at the moment of truth. Continue to check each stationery swing position prior to each shot. It is important to recognise both how your mini-swing will look to you as well as how each swing position feels.

✗ INCORRECT ✗

Left: At halfway through, the right hand has independently rotated over the left. The left elbow has folded away far too early with the forearm appearing beneath the right. The clubface is very 'closed', the face directed towards the ground at this point.

✗ INCORRECT ✗

Below: From behind, the extended right arm is clearly seen, but the wrists have independently rolled over, angling the clubface to about 10 o'clock instead of 11.30. This position is associated with shots that curve to the left in flight.

The temptation is to increase your swing length after a few successful shots. Whilst a slight increase in backswing length to 10 o'clock, for instance, will assist you in generating more clubhead speed, try to resist this temptation. The same applies to the length of the forward swing, although gentle acceleration through the hitting area may take the club beyond horizontal.

ADVANCED CLUBFACE CONTROL

The golf swing I am using throughout this section is orthodox, what I describe as a model swing. It provides a series of positions which, when linked together, form a golf swing which can be controlled and repeated. You base the learning of the basic fundamentals on this swing, but because everyone is an individual, there must be scope to accommodate mild variations in technique. Such swing variations also occur at different stages of improvement. This book is specifically for beginners through to average ability golfers, and the clubface control described is most suitable for this standard. However, it is NOT the case that everyone, irrespective of golfing ability, should conform to the identical movements. Indeed, there are many movements in the swing of an advanced player which must be tackled differently in order to maximize the strengths and minimize the weaknesses at that level.

If you look at a photograph of a skilled player, perhaps a tournament golfer, you may notice that the line drawn across the leading edge halfway through points more directly upward or even to 12.30 on a clock face, not 11.30 as described. The clubhead will still conform to the same position halfway into the downswing, but there should be an important difference between the actions through the hitting area in how the arms and wrists control the clubface. The novice or higher handicap golfer should promote the use of the wrists, working at crossing the right hand over the left throughout the hitting area. This will encourage the clubface to square up or even turn slightly closed at impact, hitting the preferable straight or 'drawn' shot curving slightly right to left in the air. With so many newcomers to the game curving shots badly to the right or 'slicing', this will also compensate for the natural weakness in the clubface control so typical at the early stages.

A skilled golfer, by contrast, will already possess stronger golfing muscles and a more developed, faster action into impact. Typically, a good player's bad shot curves away to the left in the air due to the wrists crossing over too early, independent of the rest of the swing components. A good player must allow for the faster wrist action by holding the clubface at the target longer through impact, most easily learned by differentiating halfway through between a clubface at 12 o'clock or 12.30 rather than 11.30. A skilled golfer resists the wrists actively crossing over through impact while the average player promotes the movement. If you have ever considered copying the swing technique of a tournament golfer, perhaps thinking that 'if it works for him it must work for me', this is perhaps one area which shouldn't be imitated too precisely.

The Completed Backswing

You should have learned by this stage the repetitive formation of your address position routine and a half swing exercise to move the ball forwards some 60 yards (55 m). In addition, you should be able to achieve reasonable accuracy and repetition. This mini-swing will have already developed the basic swing shape, which you now extend, starting off by continuing the backswing, initially to three-quarters and then to full length. The whole purpose of a more complete swing is simply to gener-ate more clubhead speed which will be translated into added distance in the ball flight. If there is to be a major hurdle to overcome through careful learning, attention to detail and plenty of constructive practice, this is that stage. Many newcomers to golf find the fuller swing difficult to achieve and frustratingly inconsistent in striking the ball solidly. Learn each stage, assemble the stationary positions or reference points and it will easily come together as one complete swing motion.

The Second Stage

The second part of the backswing moves the club from halfway, with the shaft parallel to the ground up until the shaft is just beyond vertical when viewed from the front. Continue the same two key movements that initiated the backswing before, turning the right shoulder further and swinging the left arm upward into the space created. All the time the clubhead moves gradually around the body

Above: Three-quarters into the backswing. The shoulder turn is almost complete and the hips have turned half this amount. The shaft is at 1 o'clock when viewed from the front, the wrists now fully hinged or very nearly so.

Right: Three-quarters back, and the shaft is past vertical, at about 1 o'clock if seen from the front. The wrist hinge is virtually completed, and the upward swinging of the arms has put the club over and just behind the joint of the right shoulder. The elbows are still fairly close to one another.

✔ CORRECT ✔

The club is now at the top of the backswing, with the shoulders having turned 90 degrees, the hips half this amount. The arms have swung upward in order to position the shaft above and just behind the right shoulder. The shaft need not be exactly parallel to the target-line at this position, and is seen here to be 'laid off', pointing a touch left of target.

on a gentle arc, passing out of sight behind you eventually. The overall shape of the swing is primarily dictated by the larger muscles in the back and shoulders, and if these turn correctly the arms will most naturally find their correct slot. Feel the left shoulder turning underneath the chin gradually as a confirmation that the backswing body turn is good.

Remember the importance I placed on the correct posture at the address position, setting a spine angle which enabled the upper body to be angled at the hips, bottom out and knees just slightly flexed. You can let the upper body move a touch to your right side in the backswing and more noticeably to the target side in the follow through. However, it is essential that the spine angle remains constant throughout when viewed from behind, maintaining the height of the head.

Checking Your Position

At three-quarters back you should check your position. The shoulders have turned some 80 degrees, the hips half that and the right leg is resisting the upper body turn by remaining flexed, but less so than at the address position. Don't allow this leg to straighten otherwise you will destroy the coiling effect of the body that will contribute significantly to power in your swing action later. The left knee begins to

SHAFT ALIGNMENT AT THE TOP OF THE BACKSWING

In the model swing, the shoulders reach a turning point of 90 degrees while the armswing positions the shaft over the joint of your right shoulder. While there is no necessity to conform to a precise backswing length, the shaft will generally stop just before horizontal, this being the point at which the left side of the body is stretched to its maximum. Differing levels of flexibility in people will dictate just how long the backswing will be. Furthermore, the swing made with a no.9 iron will tend to be naturally shorter as control is more important and the body rotates less. The swing with the driver will be a touch longer as shoulder turn is more easily achieved standing further away from the ball.

I don't think it important that the club shaft aligns parallel to the ball-to-target-line at the top of the backswing, and it certainly will not with a shorter iron anyway. The shaft will more likely appear to be laid off slightly, that is pointing to the left, which is more noticeable with the more lofted clubs. The only club where the shaft is likely to slot into the parallel position is the driver, where the longer backswing completes the swing arc. However, it is important that the shoulders complete a full turn, thus achieving a position at the top of the backswing from which an effective downswing can start. Clearly, if the shoulders fail to turn adequately in the second half of your backswing, the shaft will appear badly laid off and affect the quality of impact. One important point to remember is that the vast majority of golfers who achieve a technically correct position at halfway back automatically find a good top of the backswing. Initial backswing errors cause far more problems.

✗ INCORRECT ✗

Elbow separation near the top of the backswing is usually a result of an earlier error. The right elbow has moved away from the body as the left shoulder has tilted down at the ball too much. The shaft has crossed over at the top, and is now aligned to the right of parallel to the ball-to-target-line.

✗ INCORRECT ✗

A very poor position, the shoulders having turned not nearly enough and the left arm has failed to swing upward in the second half of the backswing. Clubhead speed will be lacking, and the correct shape of downswing to hit the ball at the target nearly impossible to achieve.

LEFT HEEL BACKSWING CONTROL

A golf swing should involve a shift of weight in the direction the club is moving or is about to move. In the backswing the weight transfers into your right side and moves to the target side coming down. This is most obviously seen in the follow through where the right toe is a balancing point only, with almost all body weight on the left side.

Weight shift must be controlled, so in the backswing you are encouraged to keep your left heel down on the ground. This stretches the left side of the body when fully turned and assists power in the completed swing. Anyone who possesses reasonable flexibility can turn fully and still keep control of the lower body by keeping the heel in place.

If you are less flexible, you can allow the left heel to lift, but it must form part of the very completion of your backswing. The heel will only start to lift as the club nears its furthest point going back, after the wrists have finished hinging. This is significantly different from letting the left heel rise early in the backswing due to a poor body turn. Work at turning the shoulders and only allow the hips to turn half that amount. If your hips turn excessively early into the backswing, the left heel rises straight away and the weight will transfer too quickly, almost certainly failing to recover for impact.

The backswing turn can only be really effective at generating clubhead speed if you turn the shoulders and resist this turn with the hips and legs, stretching the muscles down the left side of the body. While it is ideal that the left heel remains down throughout, not everyone possesses such flexibility, so the heel could rise a touch in response to the completion of the backswing turn. However, this is quite different from permitting the left heel to lift excessively from the ground, losing lower body control.

move in the opposite way to the right, bending more and pointing at the ball, possibly even slightly behind it. Feel how the body weight wants to transfer from even distribution at the address position to favour the right leg at three-quarters back. More precisely, notice that the right heel takes the weight more, in response to the hip rotation. This is very natural if you recognize how correct it is and allow it to happen in your swing.

The left arm remains comfortably extended and determines the swing radius while the right elbow continues to fold towards the body. Keep these elbows fairly close together throughout, and you will feel that the right elbow begins to point downwards as the backswing length increases. An important word here about tension. If you have adopted too tight a grip pressure or are locking the elbows in the swing, the right elbow will simply not fold away as it should in the second half of the backswing. This movement must feel light, as though you are simply putting the club into position rather than winding up for power. You will feel how the left arm begins to move across the upper chest but will not actually touch it. This left arm position allows the hands to swing high enough in the backswing and create a bigger arc. Allow your wrists to hinge continuously from halfway into the backswing until the club has reached three-quarters back. The correct hinge is the same action as when you use a hammer, the right elbow folding as the right wrist hinges back on itself. The good swing will combine an upper body turn with a hip and legs resistance to the turn while the arms swing up and the wrists hinge. By contrast, don't turn the body and then independently cock the wrists later in the backswing as this will do nothing for the fluidity of the swing and is

most awkward anyway. One final checkpoint well worth using involves a mirror, video camera or friend to confirm. At three-quarters back, continue a line from the butt end of the club shaft and see how it coincides with the ball-to-target-line. This will assist you in checking your plane and confirms if the arms have swung the club up while the spine angle has remained constant.

Finishing The Backswing

To finish your backswing, simply continue to turn your shoulders another ten degrees while moving the left arm upwards a little more, your hands now appearing just above head high. This backswing continuation will stretch the muscles in your left side running down your entire side, while the muscles in the right side are compressed.

This is potentially a most powerful position and the starting point for reversing the sequence coming down. Work hard at ensuring the left shoulder moves underneath and in front of your chin, turning fully. The hips respond further by turning to half the shoulder turn, the right knee remains flexed and the left knee points just behind the golf ball on the ground. Keep your left heel on the ground throughout but sense how the weight has moved more to the toes of the left foot, and therefore is felt mostly on the heel of the right. The left thumb can be felt underneath the club shaft at the top, supporting the weight of the club and dictating the backswing length. At this point I will stress that I don't consider the backswing has a perfect length, more a point at which the shoulders are fully turned, the arms have swung upward and the wrists have naturally hinged. For most

golfers this stops the shaft short of horizontal. If your club is short of this ideal you can always work to increase this later, but avoid the backswing which collapses the left arm or over-rotates the shoulders through loss of control. Feel that the club shaft is both above and fractionally behind the joint of the right shoulder whilst the spine angle remains constant. This is easily confirmed by checking in a mirror. Beginners often find it difficult to turn their backs on the target which is so necessary to achieve a good top of the backswing position. Use this as one of your swing thoughts when you are learning, as many learners do find it useful.

CHECKPOINTS

○ The backswing continues by combining a left arm radius and a right shoulder turn.

○ The key to a good top of the backswing is how well you achieve the correct position halfway back.

○ At the top of the backswing the shoulders should ideally have turned 90 degrees while the hips turn 45 degrees. The knees will move to a point representing half the hip turn.

○ Stretch the left side of your body by turning the shoulders while resisting this turn with the lower body. The left heel should remain on the ground or close to it.

○ The wrists begin to hinge at 8 o'clock and continue until the shaft passes 1 o'clock. The backswing is brought to an end by shoulders and lower body resistance. The wrists stay cocked.

○ The top of the backswing will position the shaft over the joint of your right shoulder and therefore into plane.

○ Limit the length of your backswing to short of the horizontal, thus giving more control for the downswing.

THE REVERSE PIVOT

Good weight transference in the completed swing is vital to hitting solid golf shots. Without it, you cannot maximize clubhead speed nor can you ensure striking the ball before the club hits the turf with an iron club. The weight will move in the direction you are swinging the club, to your right side going back and into your left side coming down and past impact.

One of the most destructive moves in a swing is to transfer the weight onto the LEFT side in the backswing and then recover balance by then falling to the right through impact. This swing will appear most unnatural, will feel uncomfortable, but you may not immediately identify the problem. I have found most golfers who make this error learn to do so by trying to keep their heads absolutely still throughout. This is incorrect, as the head must be allowed to rotate a touch and even move to the right in the backswing to assist with your shoulder turn. In the downswing, the head will appear to move as the shoulders turn throughout the downswing and follow through. The most noticeable part is at the very completion of the swing where the head rises and moves over the left leg. If you try to hold your head down or still, you will prevent the head moving as part of your body turn and run the risk of developing one of the most destructive of all swing errors.

✗ INCORRECT ✗

A reverse weight shift, which is one of the most disastrous moves in the golf swing. The weight is shifted to the left side (*above*) going back, completely the opposite direction to the armswing and body turn. The right leg straightens as the left shoulder dips ahead of the ball in the backswing, but in order to regain balance the player transfers the weight onto the right side prior to impact. At almost three-quarters through (*right*), the weight is holding back on that right side; by now it should be more fully on the left and the player's head should be more over the left leg, not the right. Such a swing will hit the ground badly before the ball, top shots and will forever be inconsistent.

Shoulder Turn In Plane

There are two important arcs in a golf swing. The first is the one formed by the clubhead which moves both around the body and up in the backswing, down for impact to brush the ground and up again to finish. This arc moves in a plane around a central point, easily identified in the golf swing as the upper chest or the top of the breastbone. The second arc is much smaller, centred at the same point and dictating the more shallow plane of the shoulder turn. The overall shape of your golf swing relies upon these two planes being correct.

You can isolate your shoulder plane by placing a club shaft across them and turning as you would do normally, not forgetting to adopt your normal golf posture. At the 90 degrees shoulder turn position, representing the completed backswing the shaft should not point at the ball position beneath you, but should instead be directed more ahead of you, appearing to strike the ground perhaps 10 feet (3 m)

away. However, your arm swing must be considerably more up and down to produce a plane which ensures the sole of the club brushes the grass at the impact point. The newcomer to golf almost invariably tops the ball because he has yet to develop the armswing in the correct plane, which initially is not altogether natural. This is exactly why you are asked to TURN your shoulders, but not tilt them. You are also asked to make a DOWNSWING, not

✔ CORRECT ✔
The shoulder turn and path of the club in the completed swing provide the two key arcs which dictate the overall shape when viewed from this direction. However, while the club swings in one plane (A), the shoulders must turn in a flatter, more shallow plane (B).

an 'around' swing. Remember that your shoulders turn on one plane, while the arms move the club on a steeper one.

Left Wrist Position At The Top Of The Backswing

You should learn how to control the clubface position at the top of the backswing, partly to confirm that everything which precedes this in the swing is correct, but mostly to ensure that the club is in the ideal position to start the downswing. Clubface errors at the top of the backswing are usually

due to a fault earlier, either the grip or the clubface control to halfway back. Assuming you have the toe end of the club in the sky at halfway back, simply swing the left arm upward and continue with the shoulder turn to complete the movement. At the top, a line running up the left forearm will con-

tinue straight, or approximately so, across the back of the left hand. This checkpoint is most easily seen in a mirror. The correct wrist position gives you the necessary clubface control which is so vital for straight shots.

If the left wrist has folded over at the top of the backswing, the

✔ CORRECT ✔

The ideal position at the top of the backswing will keep the arm and left wrist roughly in line, so preserving clubface control. It is very difficult to define square with the face, so check the left wrist in preference; the clubface will look after itself.

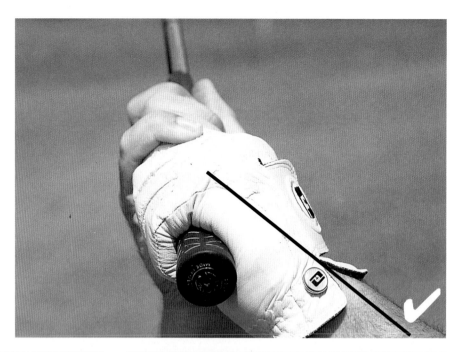

clubhead will face more skywards and the golf shot, unless you provide a compensation further on in the swing, will tend to curve to the left due to it returning closed at impact. If your clubface is wrongly positioned like this, check first that the face is not closed at halfway back, and then try to feel the thumbs UNDERNEATH the shaft at the top of the backswing.

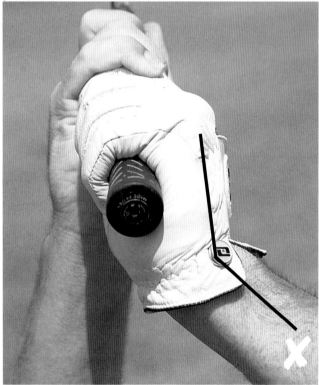

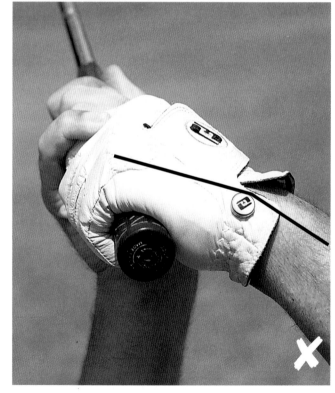

✗ INCORRECT ✗

The left wrist angle is concave, suggesting an error earlier in the backswing or at the address position. The clubface is 'open' and will require a compensation in the downswing otherwise the shots will curve away to the right as the error continues to impact.

An open clubface halfway back will tend to cup the left wrist position at the top, the toe end of the head pointing more downwards than it should. This top of the backswing position is very poor and offers little opportunity to make an effective downswing.

✗ INCORRECT ✗

A convex left wrist position will 'close' the clubface at the top of the backswing, usually indicating an error earlier in the backswing or at the address position. This will cause shots to curve to the left in flight unless a downswing compensation hides the error.

Down And Through The Ball

The downswing, through swing and follow-through are most easily learned in four parts, isolating each movement, using reference points along the way to check for correct positioning. Once you are familiar with each stage, simply link them together to create a swing with motion, one which will strike the ball solidly at impact. Remember that the objective is not to actually hit the ball, more to swing the club freely and with control so that the ball is swept off the grass. In the completed downswing, you should be aware of centrifugal force encouraging the clubhead to move in a constant orbit down and through impact. If you keep your grip pressure and overall body tension light throughout, the weighted clubhead will pull outwards from the swing center or pivot point. This takes surprisingly little effort in terms of muscular strength. The feeling is very much a free swinging motion, not a physical hit. The hit instinct is of no use to you in golf, and as you assemble the downswing movements you will notice that at no point do we actually attempt to force the shot away.

The First Stage

The downswing starts with the reverse movements of the backswing completion, commencing with a downward setting of the left arm controlling the initial stage. This is the key movement, and if carried out correctly will keep the downswing in sequence. Remember that the left arm was the last part of the backswing so it forms the first part of the downswing. Don't be misled by instruc-

tion that tells you to drive with the legs and transfer the weight and bear in mind this is a basic swing. If the left arm starts by moving downwards, the right elbow will respond by returning close to the right side of your chest, lightly brushing it. The shoulders will begin to unwind but you really must encourage the left arm and right shoulder to separate, the left hand leaving the right shoulder behind. This will move the golf club in a similar orbit or plane

✔ CORRECT ✔
An excellent first movement of the downswing, the left arm already dictating the orbit in which the clubhead moves. Notice that the left arm and right shoulder have separated while the wrist angle has been preserved.

as it moved on in the backswing, confirmed as the club shaft reaches parallel to the ground where you can check its position. The shaft is parallel to the ball-to-target-line while the line drawn across the

✗ INCORRECT ✗

Above: This first movement down is really poor, the right shoulder moving out and around far too early. The space between the right shoulder and left arm should have grown, but this has barely occurred here.

✗ INCORRECT ✗

Below: The opposite error has encouraged the arms to move freely but the upper body should have responded by turning slightly more, easily achieved by turning more from the hips. The right elbow should be more closely tucked into the body, preserving the wrist angle longer.

leading edge points to 11.30 on the imaginary clock face drawn around it. Keep checking these key points until your muscle-memory recognizes them without conscious thought being necessary. The body will have gradually unwound in response to the left arm movement, but the right shoulder is still turned some 20 degrees to your right, the hips are roughly facing the ball and your weight has transferred back until evenly distributed between each leg. The worst possible start to the downswing will cast the right shoulder outwards early on, and the arms will be forced to follow the poor swing shape dictated by the larger muscles hitting far too early. The sequence of downswing movements is critical to the contact you ultimately make with the ball and your potential for clubhead speed.

You will notice that the first stage of the downswing is principally an armswing, the body responding to this key movement. Quite naturally, your wrists stay semi-hinged, so you don't have to consciously unfold them in the early part of the downswing, nor do you hold them in their cocked position excessively long. There is certainly a delay – but positively not an exaggerated one – in the unfolding of the wrists, as this is better reserved until the club approaches impact.

The Second Stage

From this halfway down position, your mini-swing takes over, moving to halfway through. The sensation to memorize most clearly is the right hand rotating over the left, starting at halfway down and continuing gradually until the shaft is parallel to the ground level. Do try to lightly brush the grass at impact, and don't forget to encourage the right knee

✔ CORRECT ✔

Halfway into the downswing as a stationary position to check that the club and body are correct. Notice that the left knee has opened out away from the right as the hips have turned to now fully face the ball. The right elbow has folded noticeably towards the right side of the body.

moving towards the left slightly, lifting up the complete heel. At halfway through, check that the club shaft is again parallel to the ball-to-target-line and an imaginary line drawn across the leading edge points to 11.30 on a clock face.

✗ INCORRECT ✗

Below: While the lower body has worked well and the hips face the ball, the right elbow has jammed in to the side of the body far too much, causing the clubface to roll open, facing partially skywards. A square clubface for impact will be almost impossible from here.

✗ INCORRECT ✗

Left: An incorrect position at halfway down, where the hands have unhinged too early, the right hand and elbow clearly applying excessive force. Such a gap in the elbows at this stage must be avoided.

✗ INCORRECT ✗

A downswing error which is often seen as players try to drive their lower body towards the target to seemingly create more power. The legs have collapsed underneath the upper body as the hips are pushed towards the target.
They should be more fully facing the ball and ready to TURN through impact.

The Third Stage

The third stage of the down-swing sequence moves the club from halfway to find the three-quarters through position. This is very similar in many ways to the corresponding position near the backswing's completion, and the check points are basically the same. The key movements combine a right arm extension contin-uing upward as the left shoulder further turns towards the target. The swing shape will continue in a gentle arc around the body, the path of the clubhead dictated by

✔ CORRECT ✔

Halfway into the downswing the shaft coincides with the ball-to-target-line, or the golfer sees it more easily as the same line as the toes. Notice that the hips are facing the target, the shoulders only partially turned and the right elbow tucked close to the body.

✗ INCORRECT ✗
The shaft at halfway down is not in plane, and can be seen pointing away to the right of the target, instead of parallel to the ball-to-target-line. The shoulders, hips and legs have failed to turn enough early in this downswing.

✗ INCORRECT ✗
Both the hips and shoulders have unwound too early, already facing ahead of the ball. The hips should face the ball, but the shoulders should still be turned slightly to the player's right at this point. This error is very common amongst higher handicap golfers.

the whole body turn, so don't attempt to force the clubhead to follow-through towards the target, but instead allow it to follow its more natural shape. I must clarify how the left arm must fold away in the forward swing. From the position of the club shaft at 4 o'clock onwards, past impact but still short of halfway through, the left arm remains comfortably extended. From this point onwards it must first give and then positively fold away, both downwards and towards the body if you are to achieve a swing which feels comfortable and works effectively.

At three-quarters through stop the club shaft over the joint of the left shoulder, parallel to the ground level. This is not exactly the mirror of its corresponding backswing position, but beyond it a little. The right arm is fully extended and has positively swung upward, your hands reaching above head height. The right elbow has continued to fold away and is now nearing a right angle, both arms staying fairly close together. The shoulders have turned more than 90 degrees, the

left passing under and in front of the chin. It is most important that the spine angle set at the address position when taking your posture remains constant up until this point. Don't lift the upper body before the swing nears its last movement, ensuring solid contacts with the back of the golf ball. The right knee has continued to move across now almost touching the left. The weight is mostly on the left leg, especially noticeable on the heel while the right foot has released from the grass, leaving just the toe to hold your balance. Feel that the upper body is facing the target fully, if not even slightly to the left. Your hips will face the target and the feeling is that you could chest a soccer ball thrown at you from ahead.

The Final Stage

The final stage of the swing positions the club shaft behind the neck, ideally angled at some 30 degrees below the horizontal. The completed follow-through will tell you much about what has preceded it, bearing in mind that the correct downswing sequence will make each stage a mere continuation of the one before. You must strive to finish well balanced, the right shoulder staying lower than the left, but the final posture will lift as the swing nears completion, the shoulder turn pulling the upper body upward a little. This will in turn allow the head to rise and follow the flight of the golf ball most comfortably. Depending mostly on your build and flexibility, your completed shoulder turn will be some 120 degrees. The

At three-quarters through the shaft should be above the left shoulder, the right arm fully extended and the elbows beginning to separate for the first time in the complete swing as the left folds increasingly more.

✔ CORRECT ✔

This follow-through position shows how the shaft finishes the swing just behind the neck, the right arm is only partially extended but the left arm has fully folded. Weight transference has pulled the right heel off the ground, only the toe remaining to assist balance. Ideally, the shaft should be about 30 degrees from horizontal, as shown here.

hips continue to face the target, and the left leg is straight. Your right leg will bend at the knee and will touch the left, your right foot fully released from the ground with the exception of the toe. Positively feel the weight on the left heel, which will pull the toes up a touch. The completed follow-

CHECKPOINTS

○ The downswing commences with the left arm and body combining to control the movement, while the right elbow folds towards your hip.

○ At halfway down, check that the shaft is parallel to the ball-to-target-line and the clubface is at 11.30 on the clock face.

○ The shoulders will be only partially turned to your right at halfway down while the hips face the ball.

○ The wrists quite naturally unfold through the hitting area to stop the club at the next check point, hip height at halfway through.

○ From here onwards to three-quarters, the body must turn gradually towards the target while the right arm swings upward until the shaft is over the left shoulder.

○ Practise the completion of the swing, continuing to turn until the shoulders are some 120 degrees from square and the shaft finishes behind your neck.

○ Keep the muscle tension light and ALLOW the club to freely move from one position on to the next. No swing movement need be forced.

✗ INCORRECT ✗
A really poor follow-through which has allowed the right shoulder to lift too early and far too much. The right arm has not swung the club upward, so the hands are below neck height. A follow-through such as this probably indicates an earlier error in the downswing sequence.

through should be held for a moment but this position stretches the back muscles in your right side and the natural instinct is to recoil a touch. Don't force the right arm to remain extended, and if it wants to bend a touch, allow it to. The right elbow will ideally fold to a right angle, again ensuring the arms always work together and never oppose one another.

✗ INCORRECT ✗
One of the most destructive pieces of advice freely given is to 'keep the head down', so often taken too literally and causing the body to stay facing the ball instead of turning through to view the flight of the ball and transfer weight more completely onto the left side.

Practising The Completed Swing

The easiest and most effective way to learn the golf swing is to hold each stationary position so you can check each aspect, and then simply link the movements together to create clubhead speed. To some extent you can be your own critic and instructor by know-

ing exactly where the club should be at each stage and how the body is turning. Look for the angles, relate them to clock faces to assist recognition and learn good muscle-memory. The swing will never be simplistic as the movements involve so many parts of the body all

active together. You will need to be realistic in the initial stages, taking lots of practise swings before introducing the golf ball.

If you have access to a video camera, film a series of swings where you initially stop at each reference point and then assemble the completed swing. When viewing the result, freeze odd frames and apply the ideas discussed earlier to check your swing technique. Alternatively, take photographs of your swing positions from the front and back, that is facing you and from your right looking towards the target. Look at your swing in a mirror or in a large window where your reflection shows clearly. Anything which permits you to check key positions must be beneficial in the early stages.

Sooner or later the golf ball must be introduced. I would ask you to remain with the base club, a no.6 iron, to begin with. One of the best place to practise is at a driving range, so long as you are playing from Astroturf quality mats and hitting good, clean golf balls. You can try out swing adjustments and ignore your early failures, much like a skier accepting that falling is part of learning. Those who are scared to fall will progress less quickly. Start off with the ball sitting on the tee-peg and precede each swing with two or three practise swings, purposely brushing the ground away where the ball would be sitting. Keep every shot a separate item, commencing from the very beginning of clubface aim, grip and so on. Hold your finishing position to check for good balance. Once you have achieved success from the tee-peg, progress to hitting the ball from the grass or mat.

The swing is learned in stages, but must become a continuous, fluid and comfortable action. Only this way can you develop clubhead speed to hit the ball an acceptable distance. Every golfer discovers that power is not how hard you hit the ball but clubhead speed correctly applied. A physically strong man will often hit a disproportionally short distance because he is trying to actually hit, actually POWER the ball out there. His

swing technique will suffer as the hit instinct takes over, the end result being total inconsistency and not much distance. By comparison, a relative weakling will allow the club to freewheel through impact, maximizing the effects of clubhead acceleration, width of arc, a solid contact and, ultimately, timing. Timing is a word frequently used by golfers who suggest that one particular shot flew so far due to better timing, without understanding what was timed better and how to repeat it! Except for more accomplished players, I prefer the term 'co-ordination', reserving timing more for fine tuning the swing. Co-ordination is our description of the sequence of movements in the swing and how well they are assembled together to bring the clubhead back correctly for impact. The objectives are two-fold. Firstly, the well co-ordinated swing will maximize clubhead speed while maintaining control. Secondly, it will return your clubhead squarely into the back of the ball, striking solid shots from the center of the clubface.

Remember that there are two key movements in every swing, a turn of the body to the right in the backswing and to the left in the downswing plus a corresponding armswing. These are the two parts which must move in unison throughout. For the beginner, there will not yet exist that all important feel of the swing, as this is being developed, so it is easy to force the ball away by applying an independent hit of the right shoulder, unwinding prematurely in the downswing. Resist this movement, and instead work at promoting the left arm swinging downwards. At the next stage, allow the right hand and lower arm to rotate over the left. Each error will present the clubface in an open position facing to the right of target at impact, instead of square. You almost

have to wait for the clubhead which is moving on a wide arc away from the body to dictate how the upper body will respond.

Co-ordination or timing describes the SEQUENCE of movements, particularly relating to the downswing, while tempo is the overall speed at which the swing takes place. I must emphasize that there is not one ideal or perfect swing pace, and I am very much against the commonly used cliché of 'swing slowly'. A slow swing will do nothing for your attempts to maximize clubhead speed, an important and obvious part of a good swing technique. Interestingly, most swings will match the individual personality of the player, a fast person will feel most comfortable swinging briskly while another responds better to a slower paced action. Swing speed is individual, a conclusion confirmed by watching many professional golfers at tournament sites or on television with considerable variation from player to player. There are bound to be limits either side, and while the slow swing which will forever hit the ball a short distance should be speeded up for impact, the fast swing must have control otherwise the ball could fly anywhere. Your swing pace will reflect this compromise, brisk and business-like enough to generate maximum clubhead speed while actually feeling slow enough to maintain control. I would urge you to sense a positive change of pace, feeling as though the downswing is twice as fast as the backswing, but not with a sudden change, more a gradual acceleration of speed which swishes the clubhead through at impact. This aspect alone would assist lady golfers who more than men are told to slow down, slow down, when all along they should be trying to speed up for impact by encouraging this acceleration.

Developing Good Swing Concepts

Many established golfers play less well than they could because they have poor swing concepts or no idea at all of what they are trying to achieve. Golf is a relatively complex sport and the swing technique alone is difficult to grasp with any sort of control and repetition. However, it shouldn't be made harder still either by applying ill-conceived theories and the better known clichés, or trusting to luck most of the time. Considering golf is usually played for many years once learned and much enjoyment is to be had from achieving respectable scores, there should be no room for bad advice. Golf can be time consuming enough for most people with busy lifestyles, so make the most of the playing and practice time available by working with sound concepts.

Swing Drills

Improving your shotmaking skills is not just practice and more practice. You must feed the golfing muscles with the information necessary to distinguish good moves from bad, to feel exactly what a good swing is like, recognize it and repeat it every time. You will most easily progress if you isolate particular movements to familiarize yourself with them. These drills or exercises contribute to your learning of the swing and highlight exactly how a part of the body will move, starting with a simple procedure to build the swing movements.

Drill 1

Begin this series of drills by adopting your normal golf posture, bending forwards at the hips while sitting slightly through the knees to assist balance. Let your arms hang freely down beneath the shoulders and ensure they are relaxed at the elbows. The palms of your hands should face one another but not touch, your thumbs pointing ahead of you. Now begin to rock the arms and shoulders back and forth from one side to

Drill 1

Far left and left:
With your hands positioned facing one another, let the arms hang down freely in your normal posture. Keep your thumbs pointing ahead to set the important wrist angle. Simply swing the arms from side to side while allowing the shoulders to most naturally turn each way. Notice that the first stage of the backswing involves no use of the wrists, but point the thumbs upwards to the sky at waist height. Mirror image these movements the other side of the swing.

the other, allowing the movement to happen naturally, taking note that it requires little physical effort and no guidance. Let the body weight move a touch from side to side, as this also occurs in the completed swing. Notice also how your shoulders turn back and through as your arms follow the correct elliptical path around the body, this also being the basic shape of the completed swing.

As this drill continues further back and through, make sure your thumbs point upwards when the arms are parallel to the ground at waist height. Feel the rotation of the forearms as the forward swing action occurs. Sense how the right arm folds away going back and the left folds the other side. Most important of all, notice how simple it is to actually turn your body and move your arms in a motion which is the essence of every successful and repetitive golfer's swing. This is an exercise suitable for both indoors and out. It programmes the body to move through the hitting area of the golf swing – the part which principally dictates where the golf ball will fly. I don't believe this drill can be anything but very effective at identifying the correct swing shape. When you add the golf club the basic half swing will be familiar to you, the swinging motion of the arms already a recognizable feeling.

Drill 2

The next swing drill involves the completed body turn in both the backswing and follow through. When you adopted the correct body posture at the address position routine, you learned to angle the whole upper body forwards, bending at the hips and sitting slightly at the knees. Do this with a golf club shaft across the back of your neck, holding each side. Now turn those shoulders away as in a backswing turn but I want you to maintain your spine angle throughout. This will allow you to turn easily 90 degrees with your shoulders, your hips responding by turning some 45 degrees, your right knee remaining flexed and the left heel staying on the ground. With this exercise you can see exactly how much your shoulders are turning by watching the shaft. You can also focus your attention on how the left shoulder must turn to a point underneath and in front of the chin, further confirmation of a good position. Continue this exercise by rotating the upper body back to its starting point, then mirror image it in the forward turn, checking to see if the right shoulder has found its position underneath and in front of your chin while still maintaining your spine angle. The only difference this side is the shift of the weight which is made more pronounced by the right knee moving across to meet the left, the right heel fully lifted and leaving only the toe as a balance point. The last position raises the right shoulder slightly and represents the follow-through in the completed swing. The shoulder turn has continued on to some 110 or 120 degrees, the weight is felt on the left heel most noticeably, and the hips are fully facing the target.

This one exercise is hugely ben-

Drill 2

eficial for your overall learning of the swing as it promotes the correct shoulder turn and weight transference from an initially good posture. If every golfer used this drill, they would swing the club on a better plane, with more consistency and comfort. Notice that the head does not need to stay still, but instead rotates and even moves slightly to the right in the backswing in response to your shoulder turn. Indeed, it is almost impossible to actually keep the head stock still, and many golfers who believe this is important do actually move their heads just as much as those who don't try. This is another of those clichés heard often, and while there is some truth in it, I would recommend you forget this

Above and right: One of the key exercises in developing the swing involves isolating how the body turns. This is one of the most influential components of the completed swing. Put a shaft behind your shoulders and adopt your usual posture. In your backswing turn, point the shaft at the ground several feet beyond where the ball would be, not at it. Notice that impact is with the hips and shoulders partially turned to face the target, not directly at the ball.

idea altogether and understand exactly how the head should move in response to upper body turn. As this exercise moves toward the impact position, feel the right shoulder move underneath and around your chin, still maintaining the spine angle as well as your height. Many golfers actually drop their

Drill 2

Drill 2

upper body early in the down-swing as they drive excessively with their legs and hips, causing the head to dip and then rise later in the swing, a movement surplus to requirements and bound to lead to inconsistency. Maintain the level of your head and allow it to rotate or move in response to the body turn.

Drill 3

A similar exercise can be used to identify exactly how the hips should move in the completed swing. Place a club shaft across your hips and hold it in place. Form your usual posture, the emphasis here being on your rear

being pushed backwards to create the necessary angle between the upper legs and the spine. Start by turning the hips some 45 degrees in the backswing, which is easy to see and adjust if required. Now turn back to face the golf ball again before continuing onwards until the hips face the target, having turned fully 90 degrees to the target side. The impact of the ball would be made when the hips are some 20 or 30 degrees open, not facing the golf ball. The down-swing action in the completed swing will encourage the lower body to move and turn before the shoulders, thus maximizing club-head speed and controlling the impact. Ensure your body weight moves onto the target side leg fully

at the completion of this exercise, noticing the majority of the weight is on the left heel.

Drill 4

One of the very best overall impressions of the swing you can have is to simply mirror image the movements each side. However your body moves in the backswing, do basically the opposite in the forward swing. Mirror image the arm-swing and wrist hinge too, but remember that this is not a description of the swing, but more how it will FEEL to you. For this exercise, I would particularly recommend the swing being just three-quarters length, moving freely with at first no golf ball to hit. Feel the right shoulder turn away in the backswing, the left shoulder turn in the forward swing. The left arm extends in the backswing to create the necessary swing radius, while the right arm extends past the impact position. The backswing's turn in a particular plane positions the shaft over the joint of the right shoulder, and in the forward swing this position is again mirrored. Move the body weight over to the right side going back and fully onto the left leg for the follow-through. Keep this swing relatively short and introduce the ball to hit easy shots to develop this further.

Drill 3

Right: Isolate and recognize how your hips respond to the shoulder turn by positioning a shaft across them, held lightly in place. At the backswing turn completion, the shaft should have turned some 45 degrees. At impact the hips should be partially facing the target as the lower body unwinds ahead of the arms in the completed swing action. In the follow-through position the hips should fully face the target.

AVOID THE STRAIGHT LEFT ARM

I find that the idea of keeping the left arm straight in the swing to be positively destructive, and yet it remains one of the most commonly used pieces of advice. First of all, the terminology is very poor, straight suggesting tight or rigid, which creates tension and so restricts clubhead speed. Replace straight with 'comfortably extended' in your understanding of the swing.

Think of a golf swing as two sided, where the backswing is mirror imaged in the forward swing as a basic concept, with obvious omissions such as the weight transference being more pronounced past impact. If the right elbow folds away in the backswing to accommodate the swing arc and natural path, the left elbow must also fold away at the corresponding point the other side. This basic point is vital at the early stages of playing golf if you are to avoid the problems of topping and slicing which many learners carry to extreme.

Understand the difference between a golf swing where you stop at a particular position to check for correctness versus a swing which is at regular speed. The weighted clubhead in a swinging motion will pull the arms outwards as centrifugal force becomes a factor, stretching the arms more through impact and noticeably into the forward swing. However, if you wrongly try to recreate this extension by trying to keep the left arm straight, the left elbow will fail to 'give' at impact and beyond, leaving the clubface open and slicing the golf shot. Centrifugal force in a golf swing is advantageous and assists in moving the clubhead on a constant orbit or path around the body, but don't allow a rigid left arm to prevent this occurring.

Drill 3

Drill 3

Drill 5

The last exercise highlights the relationship of the armswing to the body. You will recall how the arms swing upwards as the body turns to the right side in the backswing, the wrists hinging at about hip height. This will in turn continue to fold the right elbow as the backswing progresses, pointing it downwards and toward the body. The left arm remains comfortably extended, so both arms remain relatively close to one another. In the second half of the backswing, feel how the right wrist must fold back on itself, forming a tight angle. To encourage this, try holding your inner elbow joint with your left hand to force the correct movement. Keep the right palm open throughout to see clearly the wrist folding back.

This same exercise should be used the other side of the swing, from impact until the three-quarters though position. Hold the left elbow joint with the right hand and keep the palm opened out. As you turn to your target side, force the left elbow to fold and let the left wrist hinge back on itself.

Right: Once in your normal posture, hold the inside of your right elbow with your left hand and turn your body in the usual way. Feel how the right arm naturally folds as the palm of your hand rolls in response. The opposite exercise should be used to promote left arm fold in the follow-through.

Drill 5

Understanding Impact

The basic fundamentals you have learned so far are collectively working towards the final goal, controlling the golf ball flight while developing power and consistency. Take this long game onto the golf course and you will be very successful and have great fun too! Every stage of swing development is geared towards the ultimate

Left: The swing direction through the hitting area should move the clubhead on an elliptical path approaching the ball from around the body. From here it will travel momentarily along the ball-to-target-line before moving gently around in the forward swing. Position the golf ball such that you strike it at the exact moment the swing coincides with the target-line for the most solid shots.

objectives of the impact position, and now that you have practised them, you should reflect on why the golf ball will fly in a particular way. The impact of the ball against the clubface is just 450 microseconds, during which time the clubhead travels ¾ inch (18 mm). During this fraction of a second, the clubhead will impart certain information that will dictate how the ball flies; straight, left of target, curving to the right, hit low or high, with or without power and so on, excluding outside factors such as crosswinds, atmospheric conditions and club design. Everything you do in developing your golf swing is collectively influential on the impact position, that moment of truth where you realize just how

good your swing is or face a harsher reality. Remember that an effective golf swing doesn't actually apply a conscious HIT to the ball, but more swings THROUGH impact, the ball merely 'getting in the way' of the clubhead.

Every golfer should have some understanding of why the ball flies in a particular way. These are the ball flight laws, the impact factors which you have created each and every time you hit a shot, correctly or otherwise. In addition, there is an explanation of exactly how each is controlled in your swing. This serves to confirm several key movements or positions you should have already been working at, further emphasizing their importance.

Clubface Position

The clubface should be square at impact, that is at 90 degrees to the ball-to-target-line. This is the primary direction control at impact, the swing direction being

✔ CORRECT ✔
The position of the clubface at impact will principally control the direction of the shot. It should return squarely each time for a straight ball flight, at 90 degrees to the ball-to-target-line.

the other. Golf is a game of clubface control because if you consistently achieve this the ball flight

✗ INCORRECT ✗
An 'open' clubface will be directed to the right of target, causing the ball to possibly start to the right and certainly curve that direction in flight. The open clubface imparts a clockwise spin which influences the shape of shot particularly once the initial velocity has reduced.

will never be wildly inaccurate. Clubface control tends to promote equally good swing direction control as there is no need to compensate at any stage to hide errors.

✗ INCORRECT ✗
A 'closed' clubface is angled to the left of target at impact, putting a sidespin on the ball which will cause it to curve to the left in the air, certainly once the initial velocity has gone.

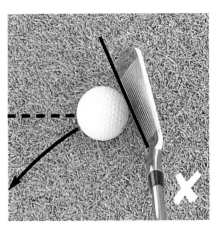

At the address position you will recall how much attention was paid to the correct aim of the clubface and exactly how the hands were positioned on the grip. When the swing motion was learned, you worked at pointing the leading edge of the clubface at 11.30 on the clock, mirror imaging this in the forward swing to again move the leading edge through the 11.30 position. Don't concern yourself with the impact position itself, but instead learn to move the clubface correctly between the two swing reference points until the ball takes off at the target every time. A square impact position will result.

Swing Direction

The clubface position is the key to directional control, but the golfer must also learn to swing the club in a gentle arc around the body in the backswing, approaching impact with the club returning from around the body before travelling down the ball-to-target-line and then around the body in a gentle arc past impact. The swing shape to the player looks like an ellipse. If the ball is to fly straight, logic tells us that the ball must be struck at that precise moment that the swing direction coincides with that ball-to-target-line, with the clubface also square. You should have learned to position the golf ball some 4 inches (10 cm) inside the left heel when viewed from the front (check in a mirror), and you have aligned your shoulders, hips, knees and toes parallel to the ball-to-target-line. These are the most influential points at the address position that control your swing direction, but in the swing motion itself you have still to position the club shaft parallel to the ball-to-target-line at halfway back and again at halfway through. These swing reference points will combine to move the clubhead down the target-line for that precise moment of impact. In addition, the reference points initiate the correct swing plane, moving the arms up and around your swing center in the backswing, downswing and follow-through so as most easily to strike the ball with power and preserve directional control.

Angle Of Approach

Think of the base of your golf swing like a saucer, very shallow and flat bottomed. This is the angle of approach you require, the clubhead gradually descending as it approaches impact, flattening out for impact before gently rising after striking the back of the ball. The angle of approach can be altered to best suit different clubs, striking more downwards on an iron club shot to ensure the ball is struck first, the turf removed fractionally after, for instance. With the tee shots, you should try to shallow out your angle of approach, the clubhead moving slightly upward at impact to drive the back of the ball most effectively forwards. There are several influences on the angle

At impact the swing must be relatively shallow or flat-bottomed. With an iron shot, the ball is to be struck just before brushing the ground or removing a shallow divot. A swing which strikes the BACK of the ball most solidly will be close to the ground level prior to impact and continue past impact in this same shallow arc.

of approach, some fairly minor but a couple worth reviewing. Firstly, check that your hands are either over or just ahead of the golf ball at the address position, again by looking in a mirror. Avoid a common mistake of pushing the hands well ahead, tilting the shaft forwards at the grip end and encouraging too steep an angle of approach to be of any use. This swing would be directed too much into the ground, losing effective clubhead speed. The opposite error of having the hands behind the ball at impact would tend to catch the ground before the ball, smothering a solid contact and also losing distance.

Secondly, the dynamic action of swinging a golf club demands that you transfer weight in the direction you are moving the club, to your right in the backswing, and to your left thereafter. The weight should be mostly on your target side at impact, sufficiently steepening the angle of approach for an iron shot, for instance, to strike the ball followed by the turf. The type of swing most likely to hit the ground before the ball would move the weight in the normal way onto the right side going back, but fail to transfer it onto the target side ready for impact. Worse still, the golfer could actually move the weight more onto the left side in the backswing and then transfer it to the right side for impact. This reverse pivot or reverse weight shift usually produces disastrous results.

Center Contact

Most golfers have a sporting background, if only some tennis, squash or cricket. Most people understand the solid, very satisfying feeling of striking a tennis ball from the sweet spot of the racquet. The same applies with a golf club because a swing which feels relatively unpowerful, almost casual in its pace, can hit a golf ball a surprisingly long way if the center of the clubface meets it. The player immediately senses how solid the contact feels and sees how far the ball flies. The precise sweet spot is opposite the center of the mass of the clubhead, and is located centrally or fractionally towards the neck of an iron club and in the center of the face of a wood. This is primarily a distance factor, as a shot struck from the toe end of an iron will lose perhaps 30% of its full distance, but will probably fly only a few yards to the right, if at all. Hitting the ball consistently from the very center of the clubface is realistic only once you have played for some time, grooved your swing technique and practised enough to have good hand/eye co-ordination. The golf ball at just 1.68 inches in diameter and the small hitting face of the club make this a formidable task. The novice can work constructively in two ways, initially by taking plenty of practise swings at every stage to brush the ground away, removing a few blades of grass or a small divot. Secondly, you can review the correct distance to stand from the ball at the address position, keeping your upper arms lightly brushing your chest and the distance between your left hand and upper left thigh about 8 inches (20 cm) with a number 6 iron.

Clubhead Speed

This is the most obvious of the ball flight laws, and is usually thought of in terms of hitting long drives, maximising clubhead speed for impact while still maintaining control. The average golfer should try to use a very similar swing for every full shot, whatever the club choice. There is no reason to vary your swing pace to influence the distance the ball travels, as the club will do this for you. Your backswing should start relatively slowly and increase gradually for impact, the sheer force of the ball contact helping to slow the clubhead speed for a controlled follow through.

Remember too the finesse shots, those strokes played to the green with less than full swings which require a variation in clubhead speed. Don't forget the putter, where the backswing length can be increased or shortened to dictate how far the ball rolls.

Maximising clubhead speed for impact for the longer shots is the end product of many influential parts of the address position and swing technique. There is rarely a quick answer for the player who wants more distance with his shots, more a long term programme of reviewing aspects of the swing until each combines to affect the result. If you want distance, work hard at the address position basics, particularly the grip and grip pressure, turn fully in the backswing and freewheel the clubhead through impact.

Adapting Your Swing for the Other Clubs

40%
Weight

60%
Weight

9 IRON

Anewcomer should learn the swing movements with just one club, ideally a no.6 iron. Remain with this club until you have developed your swing fundamentals, thus keeping the club length

The easiest way to set up for various clubs is to keep the ball always opposite a point about 4 inches (10 cm) inside the left heel. The right foot is stepped out a touch more for the longer clubs. The variation in strike is achieved by pre-setting the weight

slightly favouring the left side with short irons, therefore hitting down more and taking turf after impact. With the driver, the weight is moved more to the right to create a slightly ascending strike at impact to maximize distance.

6 IRON

50% Weight   **50% Weight**

DRIVER

60% Weight   **40% Weight**

constant and promoting repetition. If you have to work further at any aspect of your swing technique, revert to this club on the practise ground to sort out problem areas. Before explaining the difference between the various clubs in a set, let me stress that there is just one swing technique to be used which is easily adapted for the others. More about your choice of clubs later, but you need to understand the difference between their playing characteristics before learning how to adjust your stance and swing.

Clubs progressively differ in these ways. Firstly, the loft angle changes, more loft as the number on the sole increases, less loft as the number decreases. The loft dictates the ball's trajectory and therefore its carry distance and roll; the higher the trajectory the more quickly it will pitch and stop. Secondly, the length of club shaft changes, usually by just a half inch (13 mm) per club, but with a noticeable jump between the no.3 iron and 5 wood. A longer shaft length increases swing arc width, adding to distance potential, while a shorter shaft is more controllable with the more lofted irons. Thirdly, the lie angle changes, normally by just one degree per club, again with a larger gap between the longest iron and the shortest wood. This lie angle is measured from the shaft centreline to the ground level, and

dictates how the clubhead will sit on the grass and the distance you will stand from the ball at the address position. Lastly, the clubhead shape changes noticeably from iron to wood, moving from a blade to a half rounded shape.

Adapting the swing for various clubs is one area where golfers become confused because of somewhat conflicting advice offered by a variety of instructors, books and videos. The reality is that the golf ball position can vary considerably from one player to another, especially for more skilled golfers. Where does this leave the average golfer seeking some guidelines which will work best at a more basic level? I would highly recommend that you strive to keep every swing fundamentally the same, and with this in mind, I would recommend that every full swing shot is played with the golf ball positioned opposite a point some 4 inches (10 cm) inside the left heel. With the no.6 iron you will have learned to step the left heel out 4 inches (10 cm) before doubling this with the right, the ball opposite a point left of center when viewed from the front. This is the point at which the swing arc will be at its lowest, the clubhead striking the back of the ball most solidly. As the clubhead moves quickly through the impact area in the completed swing, this point also represents the precise moment that

the clubface will be square to the ball-to-target-line, and also when the clubhead will be travelling in the direction of the target, thus controlling the direction of the ball flight.

The club itself is the key to exactly how you stand to the golf ball in terms of distance away and correct body posture. As a rule of thumb with the medium iron, try to have some 8 inches (20 cm) between your little finger of the left hand and upper thigh, but be flexible about this since it will vary from player to player, mostly depending upon height and personal preference.

At the top of the backswing with your no.6 iron, the club will find a position over the joint of your right shoulder, indicating the fact that your shoulders have turned adequately and the arm-swing has been in plane. It will help you greatly to visualise the concept of plane. Think of the roof of a house, starting at the golf ball at its lower level, passing through your upper sternum, or top of your chest, and continuing behind and above you. This is your swing plane, the imaginary line which represents the combination of swinging the arms up in the backswing while turning your shoulders the correct amount. A swing which is in plane will appear to move the club shaft exactly through this line at the top of the backswing.

Swinging The Shorter Irons

I will explain how the swing adapts itself for the other clubs in the set, starting by moving to the somewhat easier shorter irons, using a no.9 iron. The club is shorter and sits in a more upright position on the ground, that is with

the club shaft angled in such a way that you will comfortably stand closer to the ball and still have the sole of the clubhead fully on the ground. I will stress that the club length and lie angle dictates the distance, without you having to remember what to alter. Simply allow the club to position your body, but respond by obviously standing closer, sitting a touch more over the ball with your posture and having your hands a touch closer to your upper thighs than with longer

6 IRON

shafted clubs. When you play the shorter clubs you require accuracy, control over your distance and consistency. Learn to alter the angle of approach a touch through impact by commencing your swing with an adaptation of the weight distribu-

These photographs show the address position and top of the backswing with a no.6 iron. The spine angle principally dictates the plane of the swing, and has remained constant whilst the shoulders have turned. The arms have also swung the club noticeably upward

to position the shaft both above and just behind the right shoulder at the top. The player's hands are just above head height as a result. A line running from the golf ball through the swing center will emerge to meet with the shaft, confirming good swing plane.

9 IRON

The no. 9 iron is a more lofted club. Its lie angle more upright and the shaft shorter. As a consequence, the club naturally pulls you closer to the ball and encourages your upper body to be angled forwards a touch more than for a medium iron. Your swing shape will feel fundamentally the same as for any other club, the club still travelling on a rounded backswing path, and approaching impact from this same direction. However, the arms will swing more upward and create a steeper plane as the shoulders tilt fractionally more.

tion, narrowing your right foot slightly and placing some 60% of the weight on your left side, 40% on the right. If you continue to swing normally thereafter, you will create a steeper strike into the back of the golf ball at impact, hitting the ball first and then removing a shallow divot.

The swing itself will respond to the address position adaptations, the plane becoming more upright as the shoulders turn fractionally less and tilt a touch more due to the upper body posture being angled further forwards, but you need not actually concentrate on this variation and instead simply swing as you would do normally. If there is to be any conscious thought throughout the swing I would recommend that you try to keep the overall swing speed or tempo fairly slow and even. A smooth swing pace translates to better balance and therefore more control.

The length of the backswing will naturally become slightly shorter. A more narrow width to the backswing due to the shorter shaft and the reduced distance from the ball at the address position combine to limit backswing length. There is less freedom to turn the shoulders and the arms are encouraged to swing more noticeably upward. Of course, a 9 iron shot is accurate, controlled and imparts a consistent flight to the ball. These are more

useful than power, so limiting the backswing length must be advantageous, even though it should take little or no concious thought with this particular point. Ease the workload of the conscious mind when actually making a golf swing, by making the bulk of the adjustments at the address position.

Swinging The Driver

Moving the other way in varying the swing for different clubs, I will explain how your swing will accommodate a no.1 wood, the loft angle now some 11 degrees, the shaft length significantly longer and the lie angle dictating that you will need to stand further from the ball at the address position. This is where the badly learned swing will show up as unsatisfactory, because the swing arc will be much wider and control much more difficult. The beginner must accept that longer shafted clubs take time and practise to develop the necessary confidence and hand/eye co-ordination, but the swing adaptations are easily made and are basically opposite to those made for the no.9 iron.

Place the no.1 wood down behind the ball which is teed up, its equator opposite the top edge of the clubface. You will have to stand further away from the ball than before, the back will be a touch more upright and the gap between your left hand and upper thigh increases. Always start with your feet together directly opposite the ball, then step off the left heel 4 inches (10 cm), the right foot some 12 inches (30 cm), turning each toe out 20 degrees for maximum stability. You will need this

DRIVER

These photographs show the address position and top of the backswing with a driver. Notice how the swing length noticeably changes, the shaft is parallel to the ball-to-target-line as well as being horizontal.

wider stance to give optimum balance throughout the swing, but now set your weight distribution such that 60% is on the right side, 40% on the left. Your target side will feel slightly stretched, your right side equally compressed. If you swing normally, the impact area will produce a clubhead which

ascends a touch as you strike the ball, driving it forwards and upward for maximum flight, bounce and roll.

As a result of your added distance from the ball at the address position and the taller body posture, you will be encouraged to turn more freely and the club will

move on a shallower plane around the body which is especially noticeable at the top of the backswing. Look for your club shaft to be positioned behind your right shoulder as well as above it by checking in a mirror. The swing length will also increase a touch, but these swing changes are not conscious thoughts but more a reflection of your altered address position. In the full swing with the driver, the shoulder turn is maximised and the shaft will ideally be parallel to the ball-to-target-line at the top. Whilst this is not a critical point, it helps you to visualise the completion of the backswing. You will also sense how your back will be fully turned to the target. If there is to be a swing thought, try to promote the smoothness of your swing and positively accelerate through impact.

CHECKPOINTS

○ Always start with a club you are familiar with which has average loft, such as a no.6 iron. This is your learning and experimentation club.

○ The shorter irons require you to stand closer to the ball. Adopt a slightly more angled posture and have the hands a touch closer to your left thigh.

○ The backswing for the shorter irons will automatically adapt itself by becoming slightly more upright, the shoulders tilting just a touch more and the swing length shortening.

○ For the longer shafted clubs, you will need to stand further away, the gap between the hands and left thigh will slightly increase and the posture will be more upright.

○ Redistribute the weight at the address position to match the type of impact you require.

○ Avoid the complexities of adjusting the golf ball positioning in relation to the feet as this is best reserved for more advanced players.

The Systematic
Short Game

Every golfer must appreciate that there is more to the game than simply hitting golf balls long and straight. In addition you must learn the basics of the short game, comprising putting, chipping, pitching and greenside bunker shots. Initially you are bound to work hardest at your swing technique, and while that is important and obviously enjoyable, you cannot possibly put some sort of respectable score together without learning to control the finesse part of the game.

Start with the statistics. The established golfer will play some 55% of shots from less than 40 yards (36 m) from the flag. At almost any level of ability, putting accounts for some 42 or 43% of total strokes played on the course. These figures suggest that time should be allocated and effort applied to this whole aspect of the game in perhaps equal amounts. In reality, the emphasis should be ßinitially on your swing technique, but as you start playing golf courses, move your priorities more to the art of scoring, more towards the finesse shots and your scoring ability will match or exceed your ball striking ability. The established golfe rarely, if ever, takes a putting lesson. Bunker shot swing technique is usually only considered when things have gone seriously wrong and confidence is shattered, making correction far tougher and more time-consuming. Golfers mix up their pitching and chipping strokes, play the wrong club at the wrong time and rely on chance to produce some sort of result.

If you are a beginner you must make a conscious decision to learn the four basic short game strokes, preferably before setting foot on the golf course, and if not, soon

after. If you are a more established player, it should be worthwhile reviewing each shot to assist your scores.

There is an incorrect way of developing your short game, a pattern followed by the vast majority of novice golfers. They might take instruction on the long game, develop a decent swing, practise, and then with the golf course accessible go off suitably equipped. The swing works well some of the time and the player progresses down the fairway. Near the green this golfer has no concept of what to do, so he asks his friend who suggests such and such a club, gives a rough description of the swing and the rest is pure chance. The problem is that this player can have no concept of HOW to play controlled shots to short distances, not without instruction or a better knowledge of swing technique and constructive practice. This type of player usually concludes that putting is 'simply down to lots of practice,' which is just not true. In reality, all the short game shots should be learned in a similar way to the swing, there being a specific technique to adhere to, practise to be done at each stage and movements to be grooved into place to remove the necessity for concentration on the basics.

One school of thought suggests that putting should be learned first, well before moving onto the swing for the longer clubs. While that makes sense from a learning point of view, I know that the enthusiastic newcomers to golf dearly wish to be hitting lofted shots as soon as possible, so I would recommend a programme of instruction or practise which tackles the short game at the same time or shortly after developing your full swing technique. Don't neglect your short game, as the objective is to return the lowest score over 18 holes and the easiest way to effectively reduce your scores is to

master the shots from less than 40 yards (36m).

The short game is most effectively learned from back to front, starting with putting, chipping, then pitching and finishing with greenside bunker shots. This is the systematic approach, developing the necessary control first with a rolling ball before progressing on to gently lofted shots, then to higher pitches and finally playing from sand. You must BUILD a short game UP, not try to condense and slow down your full swing or, worse still, tackle each shot around and on the greens as it comes, using any old method. I must stress the value of confidence in playing golf successfully, and don't think you turn it on at will when in this situation. Confidence is a product of success. Learn how to play each shot correctly, practise a little to develop muscle-memory, and good results are easily achieved. Fail because you neglect to learn properly, experience a few early disasters around the greens and confidence takes a severe knock.

When learning the swing techniques throughout this section relating to the short game, notice how one method naturally leads to the next. These are not four separate shots using four different swings, but instead a series of progressive stages where the club is used most effectively to produce the ideal ball roll or flight. In addition, notice how the swing tempo or rhythm remains basically the same, always easy in the backswing, always positively but gently accelerating the clubhead through impact. Even the most delicate shot must be played positively, with a deliberate stroke to move the ball effectively toward your target. The pace will feel very much like one-third back, two-thirds through. Your backswing length will dictate how far the ball travels, the pace of

The greenside bunker shot (left) requires the ball to be cushioned at impact by the sand, throwing it into the air.

the stroke remains basically the same throughout. Controlled acceleration through impact leads to stability and consistency with the swing movements. The optimum rate of acceleration is dictated by the backswing length. This way you will learn these shots most easily, gaining feel for the distances quickly by relating one stroke to the next. Note the similarities, not the differences. Start off with the basics of putting, become familiar with different distances, and progress from there.

Putting

The best description I know is that putting is a game within a game. It could be described as simply a miniature version of your normal full swing with a club designed to roll the ball and not loft it. For many established golfers, the mystery of putting lends itself to wonderful theories, a change of putter and much thought about what to try next. In reality, putting is simply the correct application of the basic fundamentals plus at least some constructive practice. The key objective is to develop FEEL, a non-descriptive word that suggests control over the body which reproduces what the brain has computed. However, a good putting technique leads to 'feel', but the reverse is far more complex to develop. Sadly, many golfers try putting with little or no concept of the basic mechanics involved. Learning becomes trial and error and scores forever remain inconsistent and generally too high. The formula is very simple. First of all, find a putter you like. Secondly, adhere to the basic fundamentals of the basic putting stroke. Thirdly, practise using some drills or exercises to develop repetition and lastly, take the stroke onto the course and learn to anticipate how the ball will respond on slopes and differing putting surfaces. I do not advocate

Left: The perfect result in putting as the ball is just about to drop; combining control over direction and the distance the ball rolls.

that every golfer should strictly adhere to these basics as if they were cast in stone, but more use them as a starting point. If there is one aspect of golf which is open to personal preference, this is it, where exactness of technique is least important and individualism quite acceptable so long as it works! The putter head control is critical, so comfort and balance from a stationary body position are important. Your body position can be varied at a later stage if preferred. The average golfer would be advised to stay with the basics, avoid time-consuming experimentation and keep everything as simple as possible.

Putting Fundamentals

Start with a ten foot putt on a level surface or gentle up-slope. I recommend you don't use your golf glove in putting, thus maximizing control and 'feel'. Position the clubhead behind the ball squarely to the ball-to-target-line, preferably with the sole of the putter parallel to the ground and position your feet quite close to the ball. The grip is fundamentally the same as for a full swing, but with a couple key alterations. Firstly, the left hand should be positioned more to the left than normal, a 'weaker' position with the back of the hand facing the target. The left thumb points down the flat front edge of the club's handle, where before

it would find a position a touch to your right for a full swing. Secondly, I recommend a reverse overlapping grip for putting, moving your left index finger over and outside the fingers of your right hand and returning your small finger of your right onto the grip alongside the others. These grip alterations have one clear objective. You are trying to limit the use of the wrists in the putting stroke, and this grip will reduce the opportunity the hands have of hinging more than the tiny amount needed to produce a rhythmic stroke without losing control. The thumbs must both locate down the flat front edge of the putter handle and both palms face one another. The pressure must be light if the stroke is to be smooth.

In positioning your body for the stroke, work at pushing your hands higher at the address position, and in turn tucking your arms in as you bend outwards from the elbows. The more you arch your wrists, the more you limit the independent hinging of the wrists and add to the control of the stroke. Your elbows will lightly brush the sides of your body, your feet being relatively close to the ball. I like to see the hands either over the golf ball when viewed from the front or fractionally pushed forwards, but never tilted backwards behind the ball.

Angle forwards from your waist and hips until a another ball released from in front of your eyes

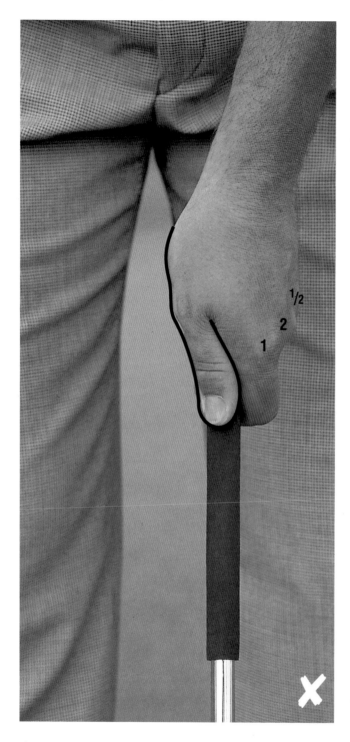

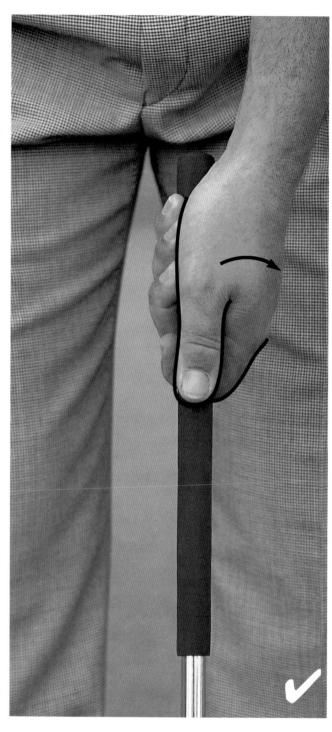

drops on the golf ball or just be-hind it. The eyes need to be above the ball and parallel to the ball-to-target-line too. Bend your knees throughout to retain maximum stability, spread your feet some 12 inches (30 cm) apart and posi-tion the ball just target side of center when viewed from the front

The left hand for a full swing is positioned such that the thumb sits to the right of center slightly, with two and a half knuckles in view from in front. However for putting, the hand is better located more to the player's left, thus restricting the hinging of the wrists and aiding putter face control through impact.

or from above. The body posture will cause the back of your neck to be roughly parallel to the ground. Check that your shoulders, hips, knees and toes are all parallel to the intended target line. When in the completed address position, form the habit of ROTATING your head to view the hole, resist-

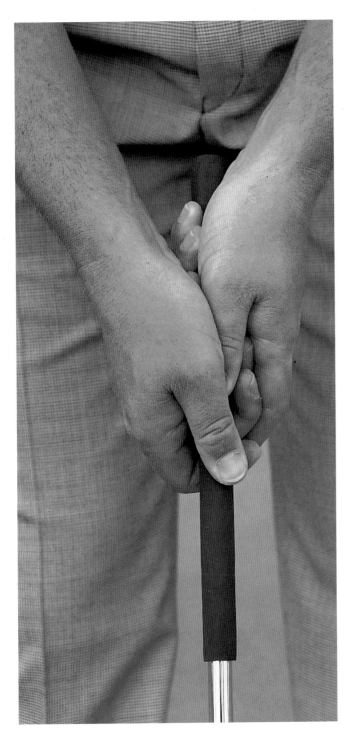

ing any tendency to lift the upper body up, thus altering what should have been correct and possibly failing to re-establish the square stance and good posture.

The basic putting stroke starts by identifying exactly where the swing center is located, midway between your shoulders or the

A reverse overlap grip is most suitable for putting, the index finger of the left hand sitting across the outside of the fingers of the right hand, stabilizing the left wrist. This is preferable to the normal grip used for lofted shots. The reverse overlap virtually eliminates the hinging of the wrists which would disrupt putter face control causing poor direction.

upper chest. A good putting stroke relies specifically on this pivot point remaining quite still throughout, the arms and shoulders working together to move the putter head correctly. The shoulders and arms effectively form a framework which doesn't change shape once the club has moved into the back-

Above: The upper body must bend more over the ball bringing the eyes directly above the ball-to-target-line. Splay the arms outwards and let the elbows very lightly brush your sides. Raise your wrists a touch to resist the tendency to hinge them prior to impact, thus losing putter face control. A ball dropped from between your eyes will strike the ground just behind the putter head, confirming good posture.

Right: The basic putting stroke involves an arms and shoulders action, eliminating any tendency to move the hips, legs and wrists. The putter head must develop an acceleration through impact to enable you to develop the stroke with some sort of consistency. Initially, work at keeping the backswing length half that of the forward swing, positively speeding up through impact to solidly contact the ball and roll it toward the hole. Notice that the arms and shoulders move around the pivot point beneath the neck, never altering the bend at either elbow mid-stroke.

swing. This will ensure that the putter face returns consistently square for impact rather than altering because the relationship of the arms to the body has changed. The putter head will move back quite close to the ground following a shallow saucer shape. It may appear to travel straight back too, but

will reach a point where it most naturally wants to move gently around the arc of an ellipse. Don't fight this swing shape which is most apparent with a longer backswing but is barely recognizable in a 10 foot (3 m) putt. However, many golfers try to artificially FORCE the clubhead in a precise

line back and this is incorrect. In addition to the clubhead moving a tiny amount around the body as part of the natural swing shape, you must also permit the clubface to fractionally turn away to the right of target in the backswing, realizing that it will easily return squarely for impact. Don't attempt to hold

Left: The most natural shape to the putting stroke will move the clubhead back and through on an elliptical shape. The putter head will move a touch to the inside path in the backswing, returning at impact to coincide with the ball-to-target-line for some distance before turning just slightly around the body in the forward swing.

On shorter putts, the deviation from straight back and through may be tiny or may not actually happen at all. However, don't fight this most natural swing shape by forcing the putter head straight back and through to the target.

TAP THE PUTTER HEAD TO RELEASE TENSION

Good putting requires light grip pressure and a fairly relaxed body. Tight muscles cannot move the putter back and through smoothly enough to roll the ball consistently to the hole. If you tend to freeze over the ball and tighten up, you can free this tension by lightly tapping the putter head, moving it imperceptibly up and down at the address position. This doesn't involve pressing anything down behind the ball. As a pre-swing exercise it helps to keep the whole address position from locking up, in exactly the same way that golfers move or 'waggle' their irons or wooden clubs prior to a full swing.

the clubface squarely to the target line throughout as this will disrupt the linking up of the shoulders and arms, the key to a solid and consistent strike. At the completion of a backswing length of some 6 inches (15 cm), feel the wrists are firm but without applying pressure. The forward stroke consists of returning the club for impact and mirror imaging the stroke the other side, the key difference being the change of pace, gently accelerating the putter head through to 12 inches (30 cm) in the forward stroke. Promote a measured stroke incorporating a change in pace, the backswing being smooth and easy, the forward stroke deliberate and controlled. The change in direction as the putter moves into the forward stroke will involve a minute hinge of the wrists which provides some fluidity to the stroke and prevents the action becoming robotic. A smoother stroke provides more control over the putter face.

75%
Weight

25%
Weight

✗

Commonly seen and yet one of the most disruptive of all putting stroke errors. The body posture has lifted very quickly after impact, the shoulders spinning to partially face the target, the weight moving onto the right side.

STRAIGHT BACK OR AN INSIDE PATH?

Many golfers try to move the putter head on a straight line back from the ball in putting. They believe this will result in more control and less deviation from the target line and more putts holed. However, this can only occur on a very short putt, where the backswing length is so short there is no deviation. At all other times the putter should follow the most natural path, because fighting this can cause problems. A putting action is a miniature golf swing, and must adhere to the normal shape even though the stance is significantly different. Although the backswing will move the putter head just slightly to the inside going back, it will consistently return correctly for impact. At least this way you are conforming to the same principles throughout your entire golf game, not changing the method significantly from one shot to another.

Longer putts also require a swing arc gently around the body as it is most awkward to swing straight back very far. Do you therefore use two different putting strokes, one for shorter putts and another for longer ones? Surely it is easier to work with just one. Don't force the putter head straight back but instead allow it to follow its more natural shape.

Try an exercise to assist you in forming the correct body posture with a putter. Stand more upright, raise your wrists upwards having held the putter lightly with the reverse overlap grip. Now fold your arms outwards at the elbows, while also allowing your upper arms to lightly brush your sides. If you now lower your upper body over the ball, you will be in the ideal posture for the putting stroke.

Varying Putting Distances

Initially you must develop your basic putting stroke around just one distance, ideally 10 feet (3 m) away from the hole. Our model putting stroke moved the clubhead back 6 inches (15 cm), through 12 inches (30 cm) with attention focused on a positive, gently accelerating forward stroke. Now I will

THE OPTIMUM PUTTING STROKE PACE

The average golfer needs to be quite specific about moving the putter head back a relatively short distance before gently accelerating through impact. Think about it as one-third back, two-thirds through. The putter will move back half the length of the forward swing which will promote the optimum pace for the stroke. Successful putting relies on you controlling how far the ball will roll, which is reliant upon you judging principally the speed of the putting surface and the contours. Imagine how complex it would be if you had to further compute an inconsistent stroke. Think how bad you could be if the ball left the putter face at impact at various speeds because your stroke kept changing. Good putting demands that you achieve consistency with this vital point. The one-third back and two-thirds through putting stroke will take practice, but it enables you to better control the contact. The biggest mistake I see is the putter travelling too far back before it is slowed down for impact. Deceleration of putter head speed is a recipe for inconsistency, and it must be avoided. Be aware of the opposite extreme too, swinging the club very short back and having to rush at the ball to roll it up to the hole. The perfect stroke will encourage gentle but positive

acceleration, whatever the length of putt you are facing. The feeling to develop is one which links your armswing to a rocking movement of the shoulders, the left dropping slightly in the backswing as the right lifts and the reverse in the forward stroke. If the shoulders don't move, the arms must be extending or compressing to compensate, working independently from your body and inconsistency is very likely. While you are working to move from your pivot point, try also to keep your lower body and head absolutely still. The putting stroke movements must be purely from the pivot point, not involving the rest of the body if your stroke is to ever be reliable.

Hold your through-swing each time and learn to complete the stroke without lifting your head or moving your shoulders toward the hole. Try to just miss brushing the grass through impact, as you don't want to catch ground and disrupt the strike. To assist this, hold with a fairly light grip pressure and don't press downwards on the putter head at the address position but instead allow it to lightly rest. Once you have taken many practise swings to develop your basic putting stroke, position yourself to play the ball. The intention is not to 'hit' the ball as such, more to roll it toward the hole.

CONTROLLING THE PUTTER FACE

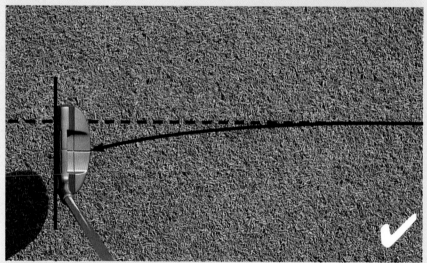

As a reasonable guide, the putter face at the moment of impact will dictate 90% of the direction of the putt, while the swing direction will have perhaps a 10% influence. Good direction in putting demands clubface control above all else, so this is the focus of your attention. You should appreciate exactly how the putter face should move through impact to enable you to develop maximum control and therefore improve your results.

While it is obvious that the putter follows a gentle arc of an ellipse, the position of the putter face throughout the stroke is not necessarily square to this path. It seems logical to move the arms and shoulders back and through, and the putter face follows the most natural path, turning just slightly away from square to the target in the backswing, moving down the ball-to-target-line at impact before mirror imaging in the forward stroke. However, with the left hand placed more to the left on the grip than with the full swing, the putter face will not remain precisely at 90 degrees to the path. It will in the backswing, but through impact and into the follow-through the left wrist holds more steady and keeps the putter face facing the hole longer. This is an advantage because it gives less chance of deviation from square at the point of impact, and the left hand position resists any tendency to introduce the wrists, which would disrupt control. Although the path of the stroke is elliptical, the putter face will seem to move more toward the hole in the through swing.

✗

✗ INCORRECT ✗
One of the most common putting errors is when the putter is forced straight back from the ball, disrupting the most natural shape of stroke. Done to an extreme, the right elbow will move away from the body in the backswing, losing control over the putter face and stability in the stroke. Straight back and through applies for very short putts only.

explain how to vary this basic stroke for different distances, giving you a simple method of judging distances for your putting stroke on the golf course later. The key CONSTANT is the rate of acceleration, which I emphasize is gentle but positive. The key VARIABLE is backswing length. Try a putt of 20 feet (6 m). Take your putter head back some 9 inches (23 cm), and accelerate through to double that. The rate of acceleration is the same, but more putter head speed is developed from the longer backswing. Move to a 30 foot (9 m) putt, trying with a 12 inch (30 cm) backswing and double this in the forward stroke, still maintaining the same rate of acceleration. The ball will roll further. You now possess the essential control over how far your ball will run, and can eventually fine tune this for the variations in contour and speed of the greens which are bound to vary from one course to another. This suggests the distances the putter moves for a set length of putt but can only be offered as a guideline.

You will fine tune this basic concept as you progress with learning how to putt consistently well, and perhaps amend it to best suit your individual preference, speed of the greens and playing conditions.

CHECKPOINTS

❍ At all levels, putting should represent 42 or 43% of the game, so enabling you to analyze your results and focus attention where applicable.

❍ Find a putter you like, based on quality of manufacture. It should have the ideal loft angle, a flat front edge to the grip and your personal approval of its visual appearance and weight.

❍ Remember that the putter's length can be easily adjusted to better suit your height or preferred putting style.

❍ A ten foot putt is the ideal learning distance when practising putting. It gives you a stroke which is long enough to judge how the putter is moving while still having control over a relatively small swing.

❍ Adopt the standard putting grip, the left hand positioned to the left of normal to restrict the chance of the left wrist hinging.

❍ The right hand must be positioned with the palm facing the target as this will help to control the direction.

❍ Find a body posture which raises the wrists, folds the elbows away to your sides and brings the upper body more over the ball.

❍ The basic putting stroke originates from the arms and shoulders and avoids any use of the lower body which should be kept quite still throughout.

❍ Don't force the putter straight back but instead allow it to follow its more natural shape. Even if this 'feels' or looks straight back, it probably won't be.

❍ Restrict your backswing length in order to positively accelerate through impact, so controlling the distance the ball rolls.

❍ Shorten or lengthen your backswing length to enable the ball to roll different distances. This method is preferable to relying on 'feel' alone.

The Basic Chipping Stroke

Firstly, I will explain the difference between chipping and pitching as many golfers clearly mix the two up. A chip is a low, running shot designed to clear uneven ground immediately ahead of the ball but principally roll the ball up to the flag. A pitch shot is played with a more lofted club and flies higher, lands more softly and runs less after landing. In pitching we try to go over an intervening grass bank or greenside bunker to play to the hole.

The novice should clearly differentiate between a very simple chipping technique, using just the no.7 iron, and the far more complex alternatives which you might see more skilful golfers play, utilizing a variety of clubface lofts to maximize control by running the ball less or more depending upon each situation. The basic chipping stroke

The chipping stroke positions the ball central to a fairly narrow stance, the left foot angled out more than the right. The hands always stay ahead of the clubhead, and are pre-set like this at the address position. Limit the backswing length in order to gently accelerate clubhead speed through impact. Keep the weight on the left side throughout and encourage the right knee to move a touch toward the target in the forward stroke.

From behind, the ball is seen to be much closer to the feet than in a full swing. Hold lower down the shaft to compensate as this controls the shot much better.

The swing back and through moves the arms and shoulders together, with perhaps a slight hinge from the wrists to assist in keeping it all smooth. The swing will want to move on an elliptical path around the body in the backswing, travel down the target-line for impact and move around again past impact. Keep the backswing relatively short to encourage acceleration through the ball.

will normally land the ball some one-third of the distance, it rolling the remaining two-thirds. Obviously, the exact proportions of flight and roll will vary according to slopes, dryness of the ground and speed of the greens. The rule of thumb to follow is to putt whenever the grass between the green and your ball is smooth and closely mown. If not, you are forced to chip over the rougher ground, landing the ball on the green and running it to the hole. Don't

pitch if you can avoid it, as the shot becomes progressively tougher as the necessity for loft increases, and the mis-hits become more penalizing. Certainly, you will need to chip quite frequently on the course, far more often than you pitch unless the greens on a given course are particularly small and well-bunkered.

Start with a basic chipping stroke from some 20 yards (18 m) away from the flag. Control is critical, so hold lower down the handle

until your right index finger is almost on the shaft itself. Use your standard golf grip, but hold with an overall light grip pressure. The main emphasis must be on the palm of your right hand facing the target, as this is the key to club-face control within the swing. Position your feet fairly close to the ball, and directly opposite so that the ball appears centrally in the stance when viewed from the front. Keep your width of stance fairly narrow, turn your left toe out some

20 degrees but the right foot should remain squared off. Your left arm will feel comfortably extended and your right elbow folds against your side, lightly brushing your stomach. Your posture should remain much the same as normal, bending just slightly through the knees. To understand clearly the last part of your address position for chipping, think ahead to your objectives in the stroke itself. The swing originates in the arms and shoulders and moves the clubhead on a shal-

low, saucer shaped arc, not dissimilar to your putting stroke. However, in chipping you should brush the ground lightly to ensure you strike the back of the ball solidly, gently lofting it as it leaves the clubface. To eliminate any chance of striking the ground before the ball, you should slightly steepen the angle of approach, effectively tilting the imaginary saucer shaped arc up a touch. This is most easily achieved by pre-setting your weight distribution at the address position

'FEEL' THE LOW RUNNING SHOTS

The chipping action is quite simple if you follow the basics at the address position and then limit swing movements to the minimum. Basically, the swing is from arms and shoulders. The clubface loft provides the small amount of flight required to clear rougher grass before the putting surface starts, but it is sometimes difficult to appreciate how the stroke will feel. Try an exercise which should help you appreciate the role of the right hand in controlling the clubhead. Adopt your regular address position with your hand partly open, closing it enough to lightly hold the ball. Now move just your arm back and through, releasing the ball to make it fly toward the hole. Feel how the position of the palm of your hand both in the swing and after the release has dictated where it lands and how far it rolls. The palm must be encouraged to face the target beyond the ball release, so controlling direction. When you add the club to play the shot in the normal way, copy the feeling of that right hand moving toward the target.

To assist in visualizing the shot and feeling how the palm of the right hand moves AT the target through impact, hold a ball in your palm and just let it fly and roll while copying the stroke.

favouring your left side. Push your hands forwards to the target and kick the right knee inwards until two-thirds of the weight is on your left side, one-third on the right. The pre-set wrists will lead the club into impact, creating this descending strike which clips the ball away neatly before the clubhead brushes the ground.

The stroke itself is very similar to the putting stroke, allowing the clubhead to move on a very gentle arc in the backswing and accepting that the clubface will fractionally rotate away from square to your target. The movement originates from the arms and shoulders, your lower body and head ideally quite still throughout. The wrists may hinge a minute amount to preserve rhythm and prevent the whole thing becoming robotic. Work to repeat the swing pace that you have developed with your putting stroke, restricting the backswing length to some 12 inches (30 cm), then gently but positively accelerating the clubhead through impact to a controlled position roughly 24 inches (60 cm) past impact, staying there until the ball is well on its way. The weight must not shift to your right side, but instead remain on your left throughout,

even allowing your right heel to lift fractionally in the forward swing. Feel the stroke controlled by your right palm and learn to recognize the pace which accelerates the clubhead through impact.

While the skilled golfer can compute the variation in clubface loft, the effects of contours, the hardness and speed of the greens and swing length for consistently good chipping, the novice should be realistic and keep everything more basic. Stay with just one club and learn to vary your backswing length to play shots to a variety of distances. The fine tuning can be done later, but start with three distances, 20 yards (18 m) which has already been practised, a 10 yard (9 m) chip shot and then 30 yards (27 m). For less distance you must reduce the length of the backswing, gently but positively accelerating to a doubled forward swing length, keeping the tempo (swing speed or pace) noticeably slower too. To increase your clubhead speed for the 30 yard chip, extend the backswing and be a little brisker with your swing tempo. Learn to adjust your swing for a variety of different distances around the practice green, preferably incorporating some variation in contours too.

CHECKPOINTS

○ Initially use just one club for chipping to keep the shot simple, ideally a no.7 iron.

○ The basic chip shot will have one-third 'air time' and two-thirds 'ground time'. This will obviously vary according to the speed of the greens and the contours.

○ Adopt your normal address position, but stand closer, hold a touch lower down the shaft and reduce the width of the stance.

○ Pre-set the weight on the left side by pushing the hands toward the target and kicking in the right knee a touch. The weight should be mostly on the left side before the swing starts.

○ The swing is from the arms and shoulders, with perhaps a very slight hinge of the wrists at the end of the backswing to preserve rhythm.

○ Try to prevent any noticeable movement of the lower body, especially any weight shift to the right side.

○ Keep the backswing length relatively short and gently but positively accelerate throughout impact.

○ Hold your forward swing and check that the weight has stayed on the left side, even pulling the right knee further across.

Basic Pitching

The pitch shot is used to play the golf ball over an intervening hazard or area of undulating ground where a lower, running shot would prove unsuitable. Remember that you should only pitch when forced to, as the swing technique required is more difficult than with chipping, the ball flight far harder to control precisely. One error which many newcomers to golf easily fall into is to

use lofted clubs from quite close distances from the flag when the better choice is the chip shot. The golden rule for anyone is to select the easiest option with the short game and avoid ambitious shots which can lead to one or more dropped strokes.

The pitch shot has a high trajectory, lands the ball softly and will bounce and run a relatively short distance. Most golfers learn the

basic pitch shot the hard way, on the golf course when facing the shot over a bunker with the flagstick just the other side. In addition, few beginners have any real concept of how to vary the swing technique to create height and control, so most struggle away with several ideas offered by friends until something clicks into place. Don't follow the crowd, and instead learn the swing required, practise it

away from the golf course until you are both comfortable with the movements and have developed the vital confidence, then apply that on the golf course. The worst situation, and the one to avoid most, is to fear failing with the shot so much that your swing becomes totally ineffective. Early failure leads to a lack of confidence. Success breeds a more positive attitude and ultimately leads to lower scores.

The starting point is a pitch shot of some 30 yards (27 m) on the practice ground or beside the practice green. Your club choice will be a pitching wedge or sand iron, certainly a club with 52 degrees of loft or more. The loft of the club is the key factor to greater height and control over the distance the ball travels, but the swing technique must also be adapted to use the loft of the club effectively.

Adopt your normal grip having set the clubface down squarely to the ball-to-target-line. Check that the palm of the right hand is fully facing the target, as this is the controlling hand later in the swing. You may find it easier to hold down the handle a little, shortening the swing radius a touch to aid control. Keep your left arm extended and fold the right elbow just lightly against your stomach. You will obviously have to stand considerably closer to the golf ball than for a full swing, but don't cramp the swing by crouching over the ball. Stay in good posture by bending only slightly at the knees, keep your bottom out to create plenty of room to swing past the body through impact and your chin away from your chest. It is essential that your grip pressure and overall body tension is light, as a finesse shot demands a swing free of tight muscles and their resultant poor rhythm.

The basic pitch shot *(left and right)* requires the ball to be centrally positioned in the stance, the left toe angled out a touch for better stability. The hands always lead the club, the weight pre-set on the left side a touch to ensure the ball is hit first followed by turf contact. The right elbow folds away early into the backswing, hinging a touch at the wrists. The swing length is roughly equal sided, although remember to accelerate clubhead speed through impact to ensure a most solid strike. Notice the limitation of the shoulder turn going back and the approximate 70 degree turn at the end of the swing.

I like to see the shoulders and hips slightly open to the ball-to-target-line, and the left foot drawn back too. Turn your left toe out 20 degrees to give added stability. Position the golf ball central in the stance, the feet being only eight or ten inches apart at the heels. I like to see the golfer pre-set the weight favouring the left side, the hands pushed toward the target and the right knee kicked in slightly. You are merely setting up to the shot in the way that you want the club to return at impact, the weight on the left side encouraging a descending strike which contacts the back of the ball before removing a small amount of turf.

In the backswing, use the same key movements which started your full swing, combining a right shoulder turn with a left arm extension to set the radius. Your right elbow must quickly fold away toward the hip, folding the wrist back on itself and rotating the left more than normal. At halfway back, the shaft parallel to the ground, check to see the leading edge is at 12 o'clock, exactly vertical. The shoulders will have turned roughly 30 degrees, the hips will have responded but turned only 15 degrees, and the weight should have moved to 50/50 or even slightly onto your right side. Swing the club just beyond the halfway back position, and feel that the whole action is from the arms, not from a conscious early hinging of the wrists.

In the downswing, you simply reverse the whole movement, returning the club for impact with the weight on the target side leg, the hands ahead of the clubhead and the feeling of hitting down and through the shot. To preserve the effect of loft on the clubface and use it to your advantage, the movements past impact have to be understood and learned, as what occurs there will correspond with the best pre-impact swing. As the club moves past the ball, you must link your upper body to your armswing thus preventing the clubface rotating over. Instead, the right palm must move toward the target longer than normal. At halfway through the shoulders will have turned fully 70 degrees, the right arm is mostly extended but the left elbow is now pointing behind you, not down at the ground as in a normal full swing. The weight is mostly on your left leg, the right heel fully released from the ground, the knee having moved across to almost touch the left. If you look at the leading edge, it will point at about 2 o'clock,

CONTROLLING THE CLUBFACE

The pitching action requires the clubface to be presented to the bottom of the golf ball while preserving its loft angle to encourage height. This is quite a different movement from that in a full swing where distance is the objective. The pitching stroke must keep the palm of the right hand facing the target at impact before facing partly skywards at the swings completion. This is more suitable than a swing which crosses the right hand OVER the left throughout the hitting area.

An exercise which will assist you involves holding a golf ball lightly in a partly open hand, adopting your normal stance and posture and throwing the ball underarm to the flag a short distance away. If the ball is to be thrown upwards and forwards, the right palm must work toward the target. This right side control is the essence of good pitching, and is an ideal focus for your swing thoughts.

the clubface angled more skywards than usual.

One vital area to practise is the striking of turf through impact with a downswing which positively ACCELERATES the clubhead. It isn't necessary that the forward swing is longer than the backswing, but more that there is a change of swing pace. The backswing is smooth and easy, the downswing gently but positively accelerates to strike down into the back of the ball. You may feel that the impact almost punches the ball into the air, using a swing pace which is rather brisk but well under control. Try to

Left: The pitching stroke is used to hit a finessed shot over an intervening hazard, the ball landing softly on the green and rolling a relatively short distance. Notice how the ball is fairly close to the feet, and how the right elbow moves almost against the right side going back. The body is encouraged to turn to almost face the target in the forward swing, the left elbow pointing BEHIND the player's side, not folding downwards.

CHECKPOINTS

○ Both the shoulders and hips should be turned just slightly into the open position, partially facing the target and probably more comfortable for the player.

○ Adopt your normal address position, but stand a little closer, hold a touch lower on the club and narrow the stance.

○ Pre-set the weight distribution favouring the left side by pushing the hands forward a touch, in much the same position as impact needs to be. The golf ball should be positioned centrally in relation to the two feet.

○ The palm of the right hand must face the target both at the address position and at impact, so controlling the clubface and preserving the loft angle.

○ The swing originates from the arms and shoulders, with perhaps a small use of the wrists in the backswing.

○ Try to avoid an independent hinging of the wrists to add to the loft as this will be very difficult to control and can badly affect the quality of the ball strike.

hold your follow-through every time as a check for yourself completing the correct forward swing, and stay in balance.

The greatest error in pitching is when the clubhead is swung back too far, causing a deceleration of clubhead speed in the latter part of the downswing. This error will thin shots over the green, the ball flying very low due to being struck by the lower edge of the wedge or sand iron. This same swing error can also cause turf to be hit before the ball, losing distance and landing the ball in the very spot you needed to pitch over. The key

to good pitching is to limit the backswing length to promote a controlled acceleration through impact.

To vary distance in pitching, you simply continue the pattern we have seen with all short game shots. The backswing length regulates the variation in clubhead speed and the downswing acceleration remains fairly constant. For a shorter pitch, reduce the backswing length and learn to match this the other side. To increase the distance the ball travels, you will require a longer backswing to develop more clubhead speed but

you will notice that the follow-through need not be equal to this. The combined action of the left elbow moving out and behind you with the added upper body turn to face the target will limit how much follow-through will be made, so you don't need to force an artificially longer forward swing.

In the practice bunker, draw a series of circles to help improve visualization. The swing must remove these circles, each one representing a couple of handfuls of sand. If you can remove the sand with a series of practice swings, the ball located in the end circle will finish on the green.

couple of handfuls mentioned earlier, and you are trying to neatly remove just this shallow piece. Feel as though you are throwing the sand forwards out of the bunker because this will ensure the golf ball will do the same. You will also conclude that this swing and impact have little connection with power; there is no explosion nor a blast, only a shallow splash as the sole of the sand iron bounces off the sub-surface and continues to a fairly complete follow-through.

The Final Stage

Now you add the golf ball, still utilizing the circle drawn around it. Focus your eyes at the point at the back of the circle which represents the spot at which the club first enters the sand, not at the ball itself. The intention is to remove the sand with the same swing. If you do it correctly the ball will pop out in the process. The danger is becoming 'ball-bound', concentrating so hard on striking the ball itself, that you fail to swing freely or to clip the sand at the right place. Eventually you will be able to dispense with the circle and focus your eyes on a particle of sand some 3 or 4 in (8-10 cm) behind the ball. This will be necessary for when you play on the course later.

Adjusting For Distance

You have learned just one distance so far, a 20 yd (18 m) greenside bunker shot. The swing length necessary represents a pitching distance of 40 yd (36 m), the sand's resistance and the fact that you never actually contact the ball with the clubface combine to roughly halve the distance the ball will travel. While this can only serve as a generalisation, with sand texture and swing strength varying significantly, it remains a good rule of thumb. To vary the distance you play shots from sand, you combine a swing length adjustment with a minor alteration to the circle-around-the-ball concept. This is most easily learned in the practice bunker where you can experiment a little, and draw the circles to make visualisation clearer. A 30 yd (27 m) bunker shot should pose few problems for the player who already swings well and understands the type of impact position desired. The pitching swing would hit the ball some 60 yd (54 m) from grass, the backswing will be three-quarter length, the forward swing almost as long, but the clubhead must positively accelerate throughout, reaching its fastest point just as it strikes the sand. Combine this faster clubhead speed with the ball being located back of center in the 9 in (23 cm) diameter circle. Less sand will be struck before the ball, giving the added distance to the shot. The 10 yd (9 m) bunker shot is far more tricky, as the swing length must shorten while more sand is removed before the ball, these two factors combining to control the shot. However, in the swing you must still accelerate the clubhead through impact, as the reverse will kill the clubhead speed as the sand resists, the ball failing to clear the lip of the hazard. Practise a swing outside the bunker which moves the club to halfway back, roughly the same going through, and pitch shots to a target 20 yd (18 m) away if playing from grass. Position the golf ball forwards of cen-

ter in the circle, and combine the two to play the 10 yd (9 m) bunker shot.

Opening The Stance And Clubface

I stressed earlier that it is unnecessary to adopt an open clubface and stance, at least until the basics are understood and practised. But there comes a point at which the introduction of an open clubface is beneficial, specifically in order to create more elevation and clear the faces of the deeper bunkers. A higher shot lands on the green at a steeper angle and therefore stops more quickly. In addition, opening the clubface (turning it to the right of target) makes the flange or bounce sole on the sand iron more effective, enabling it to bounce more and dig less. If you place your sand iron on the ground in the normal way and turn it to the right of target, its effective loft increases. You will need to increase your clubhead speed to compensate by swinging back more and being brisker with your swing tempo, but notice how high your ball can be splashed out. Don't just turn the clubhead to the right while retaining your ordinary grip; instead, turn the clubhead and regrip the club in its new position. The hands must remain the same as in your normal address position – it's the club that must rotate. If you merely turn your clubhead into the open position, the ball will also fly to the right of the target, so allow for this by aligning your shoulders, your hips, knees and feet some 20 degrees to the left. The swing shape will be dictated by the body position, principally those shoulders, and will move the club on a right to left swing path across the ball-to-target-line through impact. Don't fight this very natural swing shape. The open clubface

positioned before starting the swing in motion will show up at the reference points. At halfway back the face is partly skywards-facing, the leading edge at the 1 o'clock position. At halfway through, with the club shaft parallel to the ground, the leading edge is pointing at 2 o'clock. The clubface is not allowed to be rotated anti-clockwise by the right hand; the palm of the hand always moving at the target.

Sand Texture

Not all bunkers on golf courses conform to a specific sand texture, and this will obviously vary according to the weather conditions too. You may have to build into your bunker shots an amendment to the guidelines offered so far. Up to now, I have assumed dry, powdery sand with some depth. You establish the sand texture and depth by shuffling your feet prior to completing the address position, thereby sensing the resistance at the same time as gaining a secure footing. Remember that the rules do not permit you to ground your club at the address position, so you must 'feel' sand texture from the feet. The other way to gain knowledge about how texture of sand will affect the shot is through experience of playing at one particular course, and after a while you will probably find a formula that works.

Very soft and powdery sand poses the greatest problem for most golfers, and tests the swing technique and your sand iron design more precisely. If you have a suitable flange on the clubhead sole and cut just the right amount of sand out with the ball, you will be successful. However, too steep a swing will cut too deeply, flopping the ball forwards but usually only a few yards.

Sand textures which offer greater resistance will reduce club-

A basic bunker shot with a square clubface and stance. This is an ideal stroke for the relative newcomer to golf and initially avoids the complications of opening the clubface. The swing is roughly even in length each side. Notice that the weight starts off evenly distributed, but clearly transfers onto the left side through impact and beyond. There is no additional hinging of the wrists in the backswing as this tends to steepen the swing as it approaches impact. The most successful swing will be relatively shallow, clipping out a sliver of sand with a finessed stroke. This is quite different from blasting the ball out with the clubhead sharply descending, which is a concept wrongly attempted by many existing golfers.

head speed through impact, and need to be allowed for by increasing backswing length and also accelerating more through impact. Wet sand following rain or just a heavy, coarse or gritty sand will slow the clubhead quickly unless you compensate for it. You must be very positive about this swing, really thumping the sand with the sole of the club while encouraging clubhead speed. This way you need not alter the point at which you strike the sand behind the ball. You will probably require a slightly longer backswing to generate the additional clubhead speed.

The basic bunker shot with square clubface and stance from behind. The shoulders, hips and feet are parallel to the ball-to-target-line at the address position. The natural path of the club is gently around the body in the backswing, the shoulders turned half to the right and the hips responding to this. Weight transference is initiated by the right leg shifting toward's the target, pulling the heel from the sand. At the swings completion, notice that the toe end of the clubhead is pointing upwards. While the address position is somewhat different from pitching from grass, this swing is very similar.

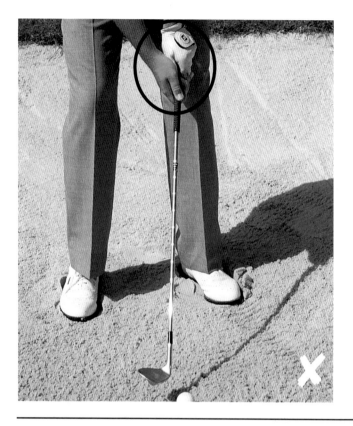

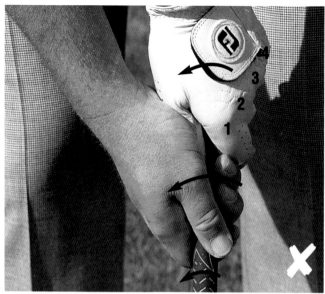

It is advantageous to 'open' the clubface for greenside bunker shots in order to increase the effective loft and maximize the role of the flange or bounce sole. However, don't just rotate the wrists to the right while turning the clubface into the open position as both will revert for impact.

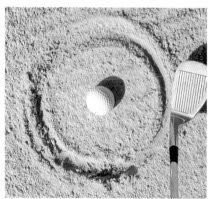

The 20 yard (18 m) greenside bunker shot with an open clubface and stance. The bottom leading edge of the clubface starts off fractionally right of target while the shoulders, hips and feet are aligned some 20 degrees left. The resultant swing will move the club on a path generally to the left of target. The club swings rather straight back from the ball as opposed to around the body. This swing shape is not forced, but is more the natural shape dictated by the body alignment. At the completion of the swing, notice how the palm of the right hand is partially facing the sky which has also kept the clubface open. A line across the leading edge would point at about 2 o'clock.

Imagine a golf ball located in the middle of a circle some 9 inches (23 cm) in diameter. The idea is to remove the sand contained within the circle, rather than contacting the ball itself. The ball will be removed on a cushion of sand, thus giving the player greater control over the distance it travels when the flag is generally not far away. Drawing a circle around the ball in a practice bunker (but never in a competition) will assist you in understanding how the impact area should be.

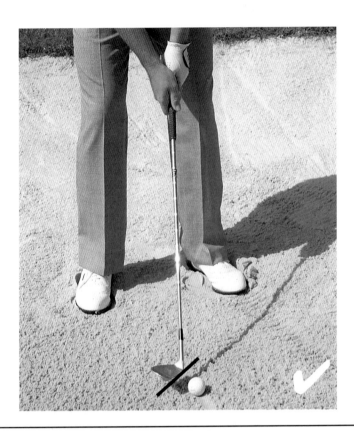

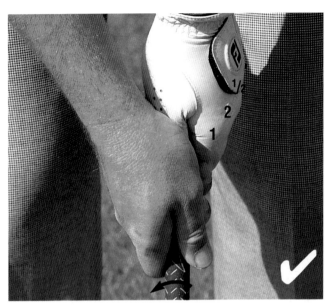

The player has opened the clubface but also re-gripped with both hands to his left on the club. From the front, the orthodox grip is seen with two and a half knuckles in view on the left hand. At impact the hands should return to this same position, the clubface remaining open, not reverting to square.

To play a longer greenside bunker shot, to a flag 30 yards (27 m) away for instance, you have to vary the location of the ball in the circle and increase your clubhead speed at impact by making a longer swing. (This is shown with an orange ball to assist in memorizing it.) The same circle of sand is removed at impact, but there is less resistance because only a small amount will cushion the contact, thus preserving more clubhead speed. In addition, increase the backswing length to about three-quarters. This will add to clubhead speed. You will find that this swing will require particular attention to accelerating fully throughout the hitting area, resisting any tendency to slow down and affect the quality of the sand contact. The forward swing may not be as long as the backswing because the wrists are not encouraged to rotate over, thus limiting the amount the wrists will hinge.

The short bunker shot is certainly one of the toughest situations to face. The swing must be positive and yet the shot must be delicately played. You still have to remove a couple of handfuls of sand through impact, but just too little will leave the ball in the bunker and possibly compound the problem by hitting it nearer the lip. Imagine the ball located more forward on the sand circle, so that the club entering at the start of the circle will have plenty of resistance to control its speed coming out. In addition, the swing length must be reduced, with the backswing now only halfway back, swinging through to roughly mirror the position in the forward swing. (A yellow ball is used here to assist you in memorizing the variations.) The swing originates from the arms and shoulders and involves little use of the wrists. In the forward swing, notice how the left elbow moves away behind the player, not down to the ground as it would more in a full swing. This keeps the clubface open throughout impact and beyond to better finesse the shot out of the bunker.

Selecting Golf Equipment

Golf Club Design

While it is important that you develop your golf swing technique as this will enable you to steadily improve your game, every golfer should appreciate the basics about club design and playability. You should know what design features to look for when selecting equipment and why they are suitable for your ability level. Many newcomers are guided by friends in their choice of equipment, often relying entirely on their judgement. A golfer could be excused for becoming baffled by the choice of clubs on display in retail shops, often described in technical jargon which does little to aid objective assessment of features which might be beneficial. Golfers are prone to make errors in selecting clubs most suitable for their game. Most critically, they fail to try out clubs before buying them, often discovering too late that they are not ideal.

Golf retail shops stock a wide range of equipment from which to choose.

I don't consider it very important that you try several clubs if you are just starting out with golf, because your swing is more likely to let you down rather than the club itself. But if you are more established at playing the game, ask to use trial clubs. The second common mistake is to buy clubs on another player's recommendation. What they find suits them may prove far less successful in your hands. The third error is to assume that you 'pay for a name' with some golf club brands, which may mean that you refuse to consider good quality clubs in the mid-to-upper price brackets. I can think of many top brands where you pay for better quality manufacture, higher-grade materials, more skilful assembly and a greater investment in research and development. If these assist your golf game, it must be money wisely spent.

I believe that most golfers buy far too many clubs initially, preferring to own a full set rather than building the set up in stages. I would encourage any golfer to carry only the clubs suitable for their ability level. Since most novices cannot easily differentiate between a four iron and a five iron shot, why carry both clubs?

Golf club design has reached a very high standard, with nearly every manufacturer producing a variety of models covering a range of prices. Many manufacturers offer equipment that can be customized to fit every height and build of player. If you are relatively new to the game, you need not form a technically sound appraisal of each and every design on the market. It's more important to identify the design characteristics most suitable for your ability. Ultimately, your personal preference will contribute toward your final choice: it's important that you feel confident about the clubs you use, as this will increase your enthusiasm for practising with them.

The Beginner's Half Set

I like to see beginners learn with a half set of clubs, maintained in good condition, all matching or at least with all the irons of the same model. The set could be made up from a few combinations of clubs, each achieving an acceptable spread across the range of loft angles, each offering the novice golfer a suitable club for every situation on the golf course. The combination I recommend the most consists of five iron clubs– namely, the 4, 6, 8, pitching wedge and sand iron.

To this I would add the 3 and 5 woods and, of course, a putter. I favour this half set for both men and women, but some men may achieve equal success with the odd numbers – the 3, 5, 7, 9 and sand iron. I would not recommend that the novice even attempts to play the no.1 wood (driver) until his swing technique is good enough for some advantage to be gained from its use. The vast majority of golfers in their early stages at the game would achieve better results using

a 3 wood from the teeing ground, flighting the ball OVER any rough which is between the tee and fairway. The meeting point of irons and woods, the point at which the ball will travel the same distance in normal conditions, is the four wood and no.1 iron. Try to avoid using either the 1 and 2 irons at the early stages, as each requires a strike from the middle of the clubface with plenty of clubhead speed to achieve good results. By contrast, with the 5 wood – the distance equivalent of the 2 iron – the ball may be hit off-centre and still travel a fair distance. A lofted wood is positively more forgiving than the thin blade shape of an iron clubhead.

My recommendation would be to select a model which can be added to at a later stage, preferably clubs manufactured by a better known company whose products are most likely to be well designed and assembled. Check the future availability of the model you are interested in, as manufacturers periodically update their product range and introduce a new design. In the world of golf equipment sales and promotion, this is essential if the manufacturer wishes to retain market share, but it could leave you with half a set of clubs which cannot be added to later. As you start playing more golf and your ability improves, you will begin to notice gaps in your clubs if you have the half set, usually occurring at par 3 holes where a missing number is the one you require for the distance. You could add to your set gradually or by simply purchasing the other half in one go, although not necessarily taking them all onto the course immediately. Many novice golfers insist on dragging all their clubs around 18 holes, when a half set would make club selection much easier.

Advancing To The Full Set

You have one of two options when you clearly need to increase your selection of clubs. First, you could simply add to your existing equipment, perhaps a half set used at the beginning stages. Second, you could exchange your used clubs for a new full set, closing the obvious gaps and completing a matched set.

The reason why manufacturers supply sets of clubs as opposed to individual numbers is to better control their exactness of manufacture across that set. They should be so closely matched that the player can easily change club without having to alter his swing tempo or technique. Even small variations in weight, shaft flex or lie angle can affect the result, so if higher quality is available, make the most of it if your budget will permit this.

Iron Clubhead Design

There are certain design characteristics to look for in ironclubs which make them more suitable for the vast majority of golfers. Firstly, look to the clubhead, which should be made of stainless steel. Beware of inexpensive alloy heads, a material which I consider quite unsuitable considering the force applied to the casting at impact. Select a clubhead design which concentrates more metal at the perimeter, which is easily seen by looking at the reverse of the head. The golf trade call this design heel-and-toe, or perimeter-weighted. I prefer the term "game improvement", describing how the ball need not be struck exactly from the centre in order to benefit from a solid contact and produce maximum distance. The vast majority of irons on view in retail shops will be of this design, since most golfers achieve better results with clubs which are forgiving with off-centre contacts.

Metal Wood Clubhead Design

The metal wood, that strange contradiction in terms, took the golf market by storm through-out the 1980s, and there is no likelihood of that altering in the 1990s. There are other materials for those golfers who choose not to move with the majority, most importantly persimmon, which is

The ideal clubhead for the improving golfer will be manufactured from stainless steel, featuring a cavity back design which enlarges the 'sweet spot' to maximise distance even with off-centre contacts.

a natural wood. A solid block of persimmon is a traditional head material for the more expensive woods, offering the skilled golfer a choice and certainly a finer work of craftsmanship. Many golfers would not part with their wooden clubs, usually preferring the less dull noise on contact with the ball and the (debatable) softer feel.

The modern metal wood is cast from stainless steel, leaving the centre hollow. On assembly, the cavity is filled with a foam which hardens to reduce the sound of the ball at impact. The greatest mass of the metal shell is positioned on the perimeter of the clubface, thus making it heel-and-toe weighted

like the irons mentioned earlier. The novice golfer benefits from this design as it puts more mass behind off-centre contacts from the heel and toe, maximizing the distance the ball flies. From the manufacturer's point of view, these woods are easier to produce in terms of exact specification. Many golfers claim increased distance since changing their old woods to modern metal woods, but a logical reason why eludes them. I don't consider there is more distance to be gained by using metal woods over woods, but I would highly recommend them for less skilled golfers. Although the stainless steel shell which forms the clubhead will not easily scuff, I would always encourage you to buy head-covers to protect the surface finish.

A modern 'metal wood' clubhead formed from stainless steel moulded into a shell, placing more mass around the perimeter. This will be advantageous with shots not struck centrally on the face.

The usual grey colour will not reflect the sunlight, and is sand blasted on the top for this purpose. Headcovers prevent this finish from wearing off or becoming scratched when the clubs move against others in the bag. An immaculate club behind an equally good ball will encourage your best swing, in the same way as a clean car seems to drive better than a filthy one!

Shafts And Grips

The golf shafts assembled in perimeter-weighted clubs are almost invariably suitable for most golfers who are developing their game, as manufacturers select components which complement one another. The flexibility of the shaft will be marked on the shaft band, so men should look for 'R', meaning regular flex, while ladies look for 'L'. At this stage I would not encourage you to become too concerned with this aspect. Recently, several new materials have appeared on the market which have been used in golf shafts, the most notable being graphite.

Graphite-shafted clubs are ideal for the average golfer. Some assume, quite wrongly, that such clubs are suitable only for very skilled golfers. However, their higher cost due to more expensive materials and manufacture put them out of many people's reach.

The grip material, design and size can be varied to suit your hand size and personal preference. The majority of grips already fitted are made from a compound of rubber and cork, offering good playability in all conditions, wet or dry, cold or humid. Any grip is easily removed and replaced at reasonable cost by a professional golfer or club repairman. Ensure that the grips fitted on your clubs are all of the same size and design, and that they are always in immaculate condition. At every golf course the world over there are golfers at every standard who struggle to even hold the club properly because they don't know that grips are renewable or, more importantly, they cannot be bothered to have them changed. This is especially relevant if you have acquired second hand clubs where the condition of the grips is less than perfect. Have them renewed if they are to serve you well.

Choosing A Putter

Retail golf shops stock a wide selection of putter designs which baffle the beginner – and often the established golfer, too. There are two aspects of selecting a model suitable for yourself. Most importantly, the putter must be well manufactured and suitable for your height and build. Secondly, it must appeal to you both visually and in feel, the latter principally relating to the weight that produces the most feel. This will vary considerably from one golfer to another so personal preference should ultimately dictate.

Don't select a putter design from the golf shop and automatically assume it will suit you. The most important variable is the length, which is easily adjusted by a golf professional to fit shorter people. Most men's putters are 34 or 35 in (86 or 89 cm) in length, but these lengths will not cover all requirements. The putter's lie – the shaft's angle to the vertical when the putter sole lies flat on the ground – may also require a small adjustment. A putter must have at least a 10 degree lie angle according to the rules, but this can sometimes be altered to match the player. Weight is more of a personal preference, but I would steer you away from lightweight putters, which do not provide the most solid strike on impact and therefore offer the least 'feel'. Consider changing the grip shape if you prefer a fatter or thinner version, and if you have a putter with a rounded grip, have it changed to one with a flattened front edge, which is permitted on putters (and only on putters) and is an obvious aid to clubface control. Lastly, try several designs, and choose one which appeals to you, one which looks good behind the golf ball, one which inspires confidence. Be prepared for some trial and error in putter selection: if it were a simple matter, established golfers and even tournament professionals wouldn't change putters as often as they do.

Additional Golf Equipment

If you have just a half set of clubs consisting of five irons, two woods and a putter, it is unlikely that you will require a large golf bag and trolley. Many golfers prefer to carry their clubs in a lightweight bag with a padded shoulder strap for comfort. Select one which incorporates a clothing pocket for a sweater should the temperature change out on the course, and a reasonably large accessory pocket for your tee-pegs, golf balls and pencils.

Shoes

I consider your choice of golf shoes to be very important, and an item of equipment which is well worth budgeting properly for if you remember that it is some 3½ miles (5.6 km) around a typical 18-hole course – and more if you zigzag after wayward golf shots! The best choice is spiked shoes, ideally made with leather uppers and a man-made sole unit. Modern materials enable leather shoes to be made waterproof or at least highly water-resistant, preventing your feet from feeling uncomfortable after an early soaking in the dew or rain. Moulded-sole shoes have the advantage that they need not be changed to drive the car home or enter the clubhouse, but they offer less stability in all weathers. Remember to dry soaking golf shoes naturally and slowly, as forced drying will reduce their life. Check the hardened-steel spikes occasionally and replace any missing ones or all of them if they are badly worn. Neglected spikes may become so worn they can never be removed, necessitating a replacement pair being purchased.

Golf Balls

Discussion of the most suitable golf ball could become unnecessarily technical, and while many find the scientific side interesting, it's of little practical help to the average golfer. Obviously, you must use a golf ball which maximizes your ability at the game, but

A two-piece golf ball showing construction. By volume of sales, this ball dominates and is the ideal choice for most golfers, offering maximum distance, and durability at reasonable cost.

also consider the prohibitive cost of high-quality golf balls if you are inclined to scatter them into the trees, bushes and deep rough to the sides of the fairways on the course.

The modern golf ball can be manufactured in three ways. It can be compression moulded from a slug of thermoplastic, which has various chemicals and other additives to achieve the optimum final finished weight and properties which make it durable. This ball is often referred to as the 'one-piece' or solid ball. It's inexpensive, will

The ball usually preferred by the more skillful golfer will be manufactured from a liquid-filled or solid core, a winding of elastic thread under tension and a cover of either Surlyn or balata.

ball, the softer cover enabling him to apply side spin to the ball to achieve controlled fade (left-to-right movement in the air) and draw (right-to-left). This ball will also have more backspin, a plus for the medium to short iron shots of a good player who is able to hit the ball long distances but who also seeks greater control over the flight and amount of run on landing. By contrast, the ordinary golfer wants more distance above all, so for him this ball type has less to recommend it. The wound ball is generally the most expensive, but this doesn't necessarily mean it is better for all skill levels.

withstand plenty of abuse and performs adequately when struck. However, it will not fly as far as other types and feels soft on the clubface, lacking that positive solid contact noise at impact. It's a suitable ball for the beginner but not so beneficial for better golfers.

Golf ball manufacture concentrates on the volume sector of the market where competition is most fierce. The two-piece construction golf ball is made from a moulded material not dissimilar from that used to make the solid ball, but with slightly different properties which add to the performance and distance potential. This core is covered with a casing of ionomer, a man-made, highly elastic and durable material, most often Surlyn (a trade mark of Du Pont). This cover gives the two-piece ball maximum durability while allowing the core to be manufactured to higher compressions, enabling it to be hit further than the one-piece.

Furthermore, the cover material is easily moulded and coloured, so improving the quality and appearance of the ball's dimple pattern. The two-piece golf ball is the ideal choice for the average golfer, offering high performance, good feel and control characteristics at a reasonable price.

The third type of golf ball design is the three-piece or wound ball, and the ball preferred by most skilled golfers and the vast majority of professional golfers or top amateurs. A small core or liquid-filled rubber sac has a thread of rubber wrapped around it under tension. This is then encased with either Surlyn or balata, the latter being almost exclusively a man-made material, somewhat softer than Surlyn and so more responsive at lower clubhead speeds and therefore easier to pitch and putt with. The skilled golfer also finds it easier to shape the trajectory of his longer shots with the balata

CHECKPOINTS

❍ If you are relatively new to golf, consider purchasing a half set from a model which can be added to at a later stage.

❍ If you have played for some time, try clubs out before committing yourself to purchasing them.

❍ Most golfers should choose perimeter-weighted irons which are more forgiving with off-centre contacts.

❍ A metal wood is manufactured from a shell of steel, distributing the weight to the perimeter and thus enlarging the 'sweet spot'.

❍ Your putter choice is bound to involve some trial and error, but remember that personal preference is important.

❍ Use one-piece golf balls if durability and low cost are your priorities, but buy two-piece balls for all-round playability as your game improves.

Golf Club Customization

All golf clubs can be customized to suit the individual requirements of the player. Such alterations from standard specification are primarily designed to fit the taller or shorter golfer, and there are certain recommendations I would make to ensure the clubs fit. Club customization is a technically complex subject in itself, and there is little point in the average golfer making a scientific appraisal of all its aspects. However, many established golfers don't realize what is possible in the more basic areas of customization. This section explains some key aspects and offers a few guidelines. Your teaching professional can advise you on an individual basis, taking into account your playing ability as well as your height, build

and swing type. One great mistake is for everyone to assume that the set of clubs on the shelf will automatically suit them. After all, we are each individuals, and we have our own preferences in addition to our own swing and body characteristics.

Club customization can be carried out in one of two ways. The more basic alterations are usually done in the workshop at the golf course where you play or have instruction. More complex work is carried out by the manufacturers, sometimes as part of the assembly of the club. In either case, there should be little or no additional cost involved, unless you are upgrading the quality of the components or requesting very time-consuming work.

Lie Angle

The angle formed between the shaft centre line and the sole of the club is called the lie angle. This will be graduated in every set of clubs such that the short shafted irons will sit in a similar way to the wood, the sole roughly flat on the ground, even though you are standing different distances from

A driver, no.6 iron and wedge all being held in their correct positions. The shaft angles vary to enable the golf ball to be positioned further away from or closer to the player while the sole of the club is sitting correctly. This 'lie angle' variation is part of the design of every set of clubs, but it should be adjusted for taller or shorter players as part of club customisation.

the ball. Golf clubs made to standard specifications will best suit the average height man standing some 5 ft 9 in (1.75 m) tall or lady at 5 ft 4 in (1.63 m). If you are significantly taller or shorter than this average, you may need to consider buying clubs with an alteration to the lie angle. The taller man would require a more upright lie angle; the shorter golfer would need a flatter lie angle to allow for the greater distance he stands from the ball. While it is sometimes possible to have woods altered, lie-angle customization is normally reserved for irons only. Most middle-to-top-quality clubs are now available with the lie angles already adjusted; on some models a choice of three lie angles is available for the complete set.

Now for the technical part. As you swing a golf club at speed, centrifugal force pulls the centre of the weighted clubhead into line with the shaft, so bending the

shaft slightly downwards at impact. If the sole of the club was exactly flat on the ground at the address position, at impact the toe end would be a touch deep. The objective is to return the sole exactly parallel to the ground at impact, which suggests that it should not be fully grounded at the address position. Your golf professional will best assess this and will look to see that the toe end is just clear of the ground prior to the start of the backswing.

The optimum lie angle depends, more than anything else, on an individual's height; but it is also influenced by the length of the legs compared to that of the trunk and upper body, and also on whether the arms are long or short in relation to the individual's height. It is possible to predict a lie angle for a specific player, but there is no substitute for the trained eye of a skilled professional working in conjunction with the player

Grip Thickness

A golfer will often comment about the 'feel' of a particular club, although exactly how one defines feel is bound to vary from one player to another. Certainly the hands sense the grip thickness as you hold the club, and this will influence those positive, or not so positive thoughts about how the club feels.

Although the set of clubs on the shelf in your professional's shop may have one particular grip type fitted, made to regular thickness, they may not be suitable for the size of your hands. As you become more experienced with your golf game,

✔ **CORRECT** ✔
Grip Size Suitable. The middle two fingers of the left hand cosily fold around the club when the grip thickness is ideal. The fingertips just meet the fleshy part of the palm just beneath the thumb.

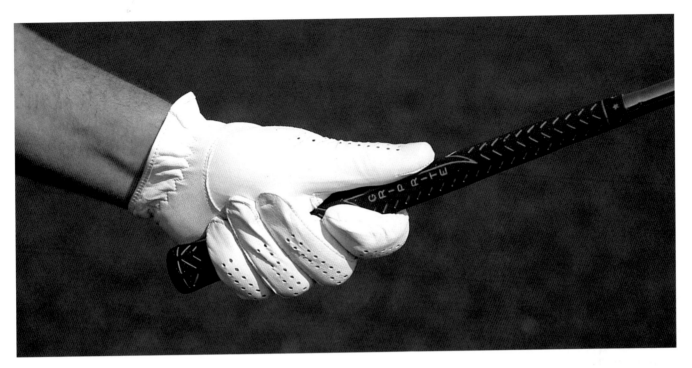

✗ INCORRECT ✗

Above: Grip Too Thin. The left hand easily closes around the club but the fingers dig into the palm. At impact the clubhead may rotate, especially with off-center contacts.

you may select a variation in grip thickness because it helps, a fact you can precisely establish only through trial and error. Golf professionals can alter grip thickness to suit your

✗ INCORRECT ✗

Below: Grip too thick. The fingers of the left hand the palm when folded around. Can cause lack of control and the wrist action in the swing will be inhibited.

individual requirements, as can most manufacturers via their custom-fit programmes. Don't assume that the grip type and thickness on the shelf is your only option. As an excellent guide to begin with, try to select a grip thickness which allows the left hand to fully close over it, the fingers just meeting the palm at the base of the thumb.

Club Shaft Length

The first point to understand about the length of any club shaft is that is can be easily altered. Many established golfers do not realize this and struggle with a putter that is too long for them and catches against their clothing, or use irons that force them into an unnaturally stooped posture. The most important quality of any set or half set is that the clubs, especially the irons, are correctly matched for length, generally with half inch (12mm) variations between each adjacent number. It is important that the shaft length suits your height and satisfies your personal preference. It is wrong to assume that all taller players will require longer club shafts, although MOST find them more comfortable. Shorter golfers may prefer a reduction in regular shaft length, but most find the standard length to be controllable. There are no rules here, no charts to read off your optimum according to various measurements taken, just guidelines which allow personal preference to influence the decision. If I am recommending customized clubs to anyone, I will often adjust one in a set and allow the customer to use it for practice. If it is suitable, the others in the set can be adjusted to match. Once a set has been customized, it can be further adjusted until both the preference of the player and the need to match shaft length to his height have been satisfied.

Shaft Type

The golf shaft is the most influential variable in any iron or wood. Its purpose is to control the clubhead and return the loft angle correctly for impact. A golf shaft must have flexibility if the impact with the ball is to feel relatively soft. The club must 'give' as it contacts the ball; if it did not, a force of some 700 kg generated by a tournament professional would have to be absorbed by the human body. Use a golf club with the correct shaft fitted in it and you will achieve your best results, assuming the other considerations of club design and manufacture are equal. Change that shaft to one which is unsuitable and you will lose distance, directional control, solidity of impact and optimum trajectory. This is by far the most critical factor when assessing

Graphite shafts are significantly lighter than steel, enabling more mass to be located behind the hitting face of the club. Many golfers find graphite shafts increase distance, improve the trajectory of the ball's flight and are easier to swing.

and the ball will fly low, weakly and to the right.

You should make a point of asking a golf professional to recommend a suitable golf shaft for your ability level and the clubhead speed you generate at impact. Try some clubs out when you have achieved a reasonable ability with your shotmaking, and assess the best shaft characteristics for your game. Ladies should choose a shaft more suitable for their slower clubhead speeds, and these will have more flexibility.

CHECKPOINTS

○ Customization is available to golfers of every standard and is a service offered by all manufacturers of clubs.

○ Alternatively, a golf professional or repairman will customize clubs to suit the individual requirements of the player.

○ The correct lie angle is very important for iron clubs. This is closely linked to the player's height, and will enable the sole of the clubhead to be parallel to the ground at impact.

○ Lie angles can often be adjusted if required, or clubs can be purchased with the lie angle correctly set for you.

○ The grip thickness must match the length of your fingers and size of hands generally. The middle fingers of the left hand should just meet your palm.

○ Remember that shaft length can be adjusted easily and inexpensively. Don't use clubs which are clearly too long or too short for you.

how well a particular club works for you. If you are influenced by 'feel', remember that this derives primarily from your assessment of the feedback provided by the shaft when your clubhead makes contact with the ball.

As you move a golf club, the clubhead responds to the effects of swing motion. Particularly in the downswing, the shaft will 'load', bending as the arms pull the club downwards at speed, the clubhead lagging slightly behind. As the clubhead nears the ball, the shaft recovers or 'unloads', straightening out or moving the clubhead fractionally ahead of the shaft line at the moment of impact. A badly fitting shaft will load too much in the downswing and fail to recover at the moment of impact; alternatively, it will not load enough if clubhead speed is too slow for it,

Playing the Golf Course

Making a good score on the golf course obviously depends greatly on technical skill. But it also depends on how you use your mental facilities to harness your shotmaking ability over 18 holes. Relatively few golfers consistently score to the standard they should, and there are many

Pre-play preparation should include some putting practice which is aimed at building confidence for the round ahead. Use three golf balls and start off with a series of putts on a level or slightly uphill part of the green.

who score 10 or even 20 shots above their potential through nothing more than poor course management.

Achieving a consistently good score on the course involves control over human factors too, such as creativity when in difficult situations, concentration, patience, self-control, and so on. There is far more to golf than just hitting the ball. The challenge facing the player is how to control all parts of a multi-faceted game. First of all, reflect on the fact that golf favours well-organized people – players

who have collected their thoughts and applied this during play. It punishes players who think haphazardly, practise little or not at all, but still expect to play well.

The golf course provides the crunch, disclosing not simply whether your swing is effective at hitting decent shots but also whether you are capable of deciding which shot to play at any given moment. If you want the best out of your shotmaking ability, strive to learn the basics of good course management. The combination of both will lead to lower scores.

Pre-Play Preparation

Be an organized golfer. You need to focus your attention on the course, its design and layout, the best way to play each hole and which clubs you will require. Your mind must be clear to think about each shot, visualize the flight and determine which club you will require to execute it successfully. An organized golfer will complete his pre-play preparation before stepping onto the first tee, starting with the equipment.

Check that you have plenty of golf balls, tee pegs, several golf ball markers for the green, at least one pencil (preferably sharpened), a copy of the Rules of Golf in booklet form, and any clothing you might require should it rain or turn cold. You should have a golf glove, but is it stored in its original package to preserve its natural texture and prolong its life, or is it dry and worn? The more organized you are, the more you can focus your attention on the game ahead.

I highly recommend a pre-play warm up. Ideally this will be a practice session with a couple of

objectives: first, to stretch the golfing muscles and warm them up ready for the full swings; second, to develop an idea relevant to the game ahead. This usually takes the form of a swing thought, something to focus your mind on such as 'head steady' or a slightly slower pace to your swing to add more control. Remember these are not swing alterations but just thoughts for the day. I would never recommend last-minute deviations from your normal swing technique – that's a recipe for disaster. Hopefully, you will hit only some 30 or 40 warm up shots, starting with the wedge and building up to the driver or 3 wood. If the golf club at which you are playing does not have the facilities to warm up in this way, at least place a club shaft behind your neck and practise your body turn, gradually easing the shoulders round in stages so as not to pull any muscles. Take plenty of practice swings (well away from anyone else for safety's sake) and brush the grass away at the impact position to tell you that the clubhead is

returning to the correct position.

Before walking to the first teeing ground, visit the practice putting green, using three golf balls. Start with some putts from 10 feet away from a hole on a level or slightly uphill part of the green. Work at achieving a solid contact from the centre of the putter face. Try to strike the ball positively, really feeling the gentle acceleration of the putter head through impact. Concentrate on keeping your head absolutely still, resist any tendency to watch the ball too quickly, even listening for the ball to drop into the hole by keeping your eyes focused on the impact point.

Make sure you have your scorecard, and if the course is unfamiliar to you, check to see if there are any local rules (usually posted on the golf club notice-board) in addition to those on the back of the card. At the first tee, make a habit of counting your clubs. You might think this far-fetched, but it's easy to leave your putter adjacent to the practice green, and it might save you some embarrassment.

The Game Plan

Every golf course has an advantageous route around it to maximize your chances of returning your lowest score over 18 holes. In addition, every hole on a golf course has a preferred tactical approach which needs to be considered. Your game plan should cover every aspect of course strategy and club selection, and should primarily be geared so as to avoid the areas of greatest risk on each hole. The key to this strategy is positional play. Avoid any out of bounds areas on the course and any patch of very dense rough where the ball will probably be lost. These represent places where the rules of golf offer only one choice, to play another ball and add a penalty stroke to your score. The next worst situation is where you are certain to lose one shot, as when the ball is in trees, heavy rough, a stream, pond or lake. Certainly better than these are fairway bunkers, where you might

be able to gain distance assuming the lie is clean and the face of the bunker not too steep. Finally, there are the greenside bunkers, grassy hollows, uneven lies on the fairways and light rough, all of which provide a challenge but are positions from which a good recovery can be achieved.

It is absolutely vital that your personal game plan reflects your own abilities and weaknesses. You may, for instance, find it particularly difficult playing from greenside bunkers, so you must either learn how to improve that problem area or avoid these hazards as much as possible. There are several ideas which should be built into your game plan and applied wherever you play. I like the term 'percentage golf', keeping the ball in play, generally hitting the middle of every green and not chancing the riskier direct route to a pin positioned behind a deep greenside bunker. The cleanness of the lie of

the ball is important, because the average player's golf swing will not be able to cope adequately with heavy rough. Avoid slopes wherever possible, as these shots demand more advanced control with the swing, more visualization and playing experience. Select clubs which land the ball in the fairway, not ones which might hit the ball 30 yards further but at a heavy price if it's off target. I don't advocate patting the ball weakly around the course, but urge you to recognize the occasions when you should clearly play boldly, generally where the fairway is wide and the rough not at all penalizing. There are also situations where you have to play a positional shot into an open area, even if it means aiming away from the flagstick a little, logically termed 'percentage golf'. If you can think your way strategically around the course, you will be able to return scores equal to or better than your shotmaking ability.

Taking Your Game On To The Golf Course

Every golf shot you ever hit on the golf course must follow a pre-shot routine. This is one vital point you can observe and copy from every playing professional you watch on television or when attending a tournament. The routines differ from one player to another, but are always consistent for each individual. A golf swing lasts just two seconds but a successful

golf shot takes some 45 seconds. Start off with shot visualization. If you cannot 'see' the shot and picture the ball's flight in your mind's eye, it's hardly worth making a swing. So stand behind the ball, look down the target-line torward the flag or center of the fairway and let your imagination form the successful shot. Good golf demands mind programming. You

have to programme the mind because it is impossible to concentrate on all the swing ideas and thoughts in just two seconds. By having that final result in your mind, it will assist you in achieving all that must precede it, such as good aim, a free-swinging action through impact and a complete follow-through.

You must become good at course

Every successful golf shot you ever play commences with visualization. You must 'see' the shot you are trying to play, picture its flight and sense the swing required which in turn programmes the mind and body to best achieve your ideal result. Stand some distance behind the ball and look down the ball-to-target-line before forming the address position.

CHECKPOINTS

○ There is far more to golf than hitting shots long and straight. You have to learn good course management to maximize your ability and translate it into better scores.

○ Become an organized golfer. Prepare your golf equipment in advance of playing to enable you to concentrate better on your game.

○ Warm up before you play, ideally by hitting shots on the practice ground and practice putting to ascertain the speed of the greens.

○ Always carry a Rules of Golf booklet in your bag and don't forget to look at the local rules printed on the back of the scorecard or those posted on the notice-board in the clubhouse.

○ Identify your personal game plan and return to it at every opportunity. Avoid the most penalizing areas on the course, such as out of bounds and lost-ball situations.

○ Always use the same pre-shot routine. Approach every shot from behind the ball-to-target-line, having visualized the shot and swing required.

○ Every golf hole has a preferred route from tee to green which should be identified before playing your tee shot. This will keep you away from potential trouble and avoid wasted shots.

management. Many a good striker of the golf ball returns poor scores because he cannot translate solid shots into low scores. However, he can learn how to gain this ability just by recognizing the situations where his shot-wasting habits come to the fore and applying different tactics and percentage golf.

Every golf hole has a preferred route which you should identify on the teeing ground. It takes just a moment to judge which side of the green offers the best approach with the least trouble. Decide which side of the fairway is safer, and if the hole is tree-lined, consider another

club choice which might lose a little distance but should keep the ball on the fairway, giving you an advantage with your second stroke. Stay well away from out-of-bounds fences and very deep rough or dense trees, as these spell trouble for the score.

Of course, there is no single game plan which can be universally applied for every golfer at this stage as everyone's strengths and weaknesses vary. There will always be the player who reaches for the trusty seven iron when all else fails, or the player who simply cannot use the wooden clubs, and the player who invariably misses those short putts. Each of these shortcomings can be alleviated in time through correction and practice, but a game plan will greatly help to minimize their effect.

To illustrate some typical problems of course management, let's look at three golf holes and think about a suitable game plan to apply to each.

Hole No.1

This is a par-4 hole of 395 yards. While a skilled player would play a driver from the teeing ground, followed by a short iron such as an eight or nine, the novice has to think rather differently. The game plan for this hole is based on the location of the trees down the left side of the fairway and the bunkers which surround the green. The best tee shot will be played down the right side of the fairway, bearing in mind that the rough is very light if the shot

Left: Hole no.1, 395 yards. Par 4. The average golfer should be thinking about the design features of this hole, with trees down the left side which are likely to affect a drive hit that way. The best line is to the right of the fairway, leaving a clear shot torward the green past the trees.

be pushed a touch. The second could be positioned before the bunker in front of the green, leaving a short pitch to the flag.

Even if the reality varies considerably from your ideal, the importance is more on programming the mind to assess the various design features of the golf hole and identify a tactical route that will assist your score the most. If you deviate from the ideal, reassess the game plan, but keep the overall priorities in mind.

Hole No.2

The second is a par-3 hole measuring 155 yards. The lake to the right side of the green also covers part of the front and obviously dictates the tactical approach. The percentage shot will be aimed at the left side of the green, permitting even a slightly pushed shot to the right to land on the green or before it. Avoid the bold shot straight at the flag, as this offers virtually no room for error if pushed or sliced.

The other design feature clearly visible from the teeing ground is the contouring to the back left-hand side, suggesting that a shot landing pin high or short of the green will offer a clear putt or chip and run. If the tee shot is even slightly long, the sloping ground will force you to pitch back over the

Left: Hole no.2, 155 yards. Par 3. The difficulty of the pin position and location of the lake to the right and before the green suggest the safest tee shot is aimed to the left side, ideally short of the sloping ground pin high and beyond.

grassed bank or play from an uneven stance, adding difficulty.

Hole No.3

The third example is a long hole, a par-5 of 506 yards. It is more difficult to settle on a specific route on many long holes because often you cannot clearly see the layout and hazards of the more distant parts of the fairway from the tee. However, you can still determine a basic route from point to point.

This particular hole features a gently dipping and then gradually rising fairway, which for the tee shot is bordered by trees on the right and rough on the left. The aiming point is just left of center,

played with a 3 wood. Play your second shot to just short of the cross bunkers, which are some 120 yards before the green. The third shot might be a medium or short iron as there are no bunkers around the green to consider. If your ball lands in a fairway bunker, the first objective is to return it to a level stance position for your next stroke, taking care not to compound a small mistake by being over ambitious and going for too much length.

Hole no.3, 506 yards. Par 5. A tee shot just left of center will encourage the most suitable second played short of the fairway bunkers located some 120 yards (108 m) before the green. This is the best route for this golf hole design, staying away from trouble which would cause dropped shots.

Errors and Corrections

To err is human. Even the finest tournament pros mis-hit the ball occasionally or miscalculate the line or distance of their shots. One of the commonest sights at tournaments is that of a player on the practice ground having some aspect of his swing checked by a fellow pro. For the newcomer to golf, falling into bad habits with swing technique is all part of the learning process. How he analyses any error and sets about correcting it can make a significant difference to his performance and enjoyment of the game.

In your first few years of playing golf, you are most likely to let swing errors creep in. You are still building your muscle-memory, that

Left: Directional errors fall into four categories: the 'pushed' shot flies straight but to the right of target, the 'pull' flies straight but to the left and shots which curve right are 'sliced' and left 'hooked'.

unconscious control of the movements that eliminates having to think about every detail of the swing. Your swing must eventually become automatic, but the difficulty and exactness of it demands that you constantly apply sound concepts until the end product is successful. Become knowledgeable about the basic fundamentals, adhere to them through thick and thin and practise the correct movements until they occur without conscious thought.

Golf can be described as a game of errors, and your score will reflect how well you avoid them and keep the ball in play. The golf swing need vary only slightly from the ideal to cause a bad shot; this exactness of technique and repetition is part of the intrigue and challenge of the game.

The point to stress is that any swing error needs to be identified, analysed and corrected before you

compound the problem by spending time and effort grooving it into place. Most swing errors are easily identified and solved with relatively little practice if tackled before the error becomes built into the muscle-memory. Bad golfers who constantly struggle with various swing problems may devote much time and effort to error correction; but it is the quality of learning, not numbers of practice balls hit, which will make the difference. Don't let the golf swing baffle you. It's not particularly complex if analysed correctly. Error correction will often require that you seek the assistance of a skilled golf instructor, someone able to pinpoint exactly what you do both correctly and wrongly in the swing. Become knowledgeable about your golf swing and then set about hitting practice balls in a constructive manner to retrain that muscle-memory.

Topping and Thin Shots

In a topped shot the leading edge of the clubface strikes above the equator of the ball. The ball is driven partly into the ground because the loft angle on the clubface is ineffective at striking the shot into the air. The ball will bounce forwards or roll, depending upon the severity of the mis-hit, and often will travel only a short distance. A thinned shot is when the leading edge strikes the very middle of the ball, causing a low shot which usually lacks distance. However, if you hit a thin shot when attempting a pitch with a lofted club, the low trajectory may fire the ball over the green instead of lofting it high so that it finishes by the hole.

If you are new to golf, both these errors can cause problems.

Remember that the ball is a small object to be struck with the clubhead, and it sits on the ground or very close to it if teed up. The clubhead must brush the ground away or even remove a small amount of turf in the process. There are two impacts in a good swing. One is the clubhead striking the back of the ball and the other is the sole of the club brushing the grass and almost thumping the ground at its lowest point in the arc. I like to see beginners taking lots of practice swings, but not hitting too many balls. Develop the swinging action by *not* having an object to hit forwards, so you can work on making the club strike the ground at the point just left of center in relation to the feet. Many

golfers seem to think that this should occur automatically if the club starts back correctly from the address position, but I believe it must be learned. What you are developing is hand/eye co-ordination. You are learning to control a clubhead quite precisely, and that will require much practice. Don't take practice swings which pass over the ground, as this will create the problem or make it worse. Instead, take every opportunity you have to practice swing with a purpose, and in this case return the club to brush the ground.

You may have to look further at the basic fundamentals for the correction. The completed swing will move the clubhead in an orbit around a swing center. Your body must have a central point which forms the axis of the turn. Your spine is the axis around which your upper body rotates. The center of your swing is, the top of your sternum, the middle point between your shoulders. In your complete swing the shoulders will turn some 90 degrees in the backswing and slightly further in the downswing, and you must keep the angle of the spine constant throughout. It is only at the completion of the follow-through that the spine is nearly vertical. Until that point it should maintain the angle adopted at address.

The main swing arc is traced by the clubhead. At address and until the clubhead has passed through the impact area the left arm should be more or less straight – but *not* locked at the elbow. The line made by your left arm and the club shaft

dictates the radius of the circle described by the clubhead during the course of the complete swing. The club remains on this wide arc dictated by the left arm radius until the right arm takes over beyond the impact area. In other words, your swing has a center and a radius and if both remain constant throughout, ball contact *must* be solid and the clubhead *must* brush the ground at impact.

Maintaining the Spine Angle

When practising you should check your posture and how you turn your body in your swing. Return to the address position and remind yourself of the body posture from which you swing most effectively. You have to bend at the hips, forming a positive angle between the spine and upper legs. This will initially feel as though your bottom is pushed backwards. Flex the knees slightly to assist balance, and feel that your weight is evenly distributed between toes and heels. Your chin must be up and away from your chest to enable a good shoulder turn. Your arms should hang freely downwards from your shoulders, allowing an angle to form at the wrists between the shaft and arms.

From here you swing back and through by turning the shoulders around the angled pivot of your spine. You must remain in this posture throughout the swing,

until the ball is in flight. Only at the completion of the follow-through will the body posture lift to complete the swing. You can isolate your body posture and turn by placing a club shaft behind your neck and holding it in place on either side. Form your posture and practise your turn to see if you can keep your spine angle constant. Notice particularly how the left shoulder moves underneath and in front of your chin in the backswing turn while the right shoulder does the same in the through swing. The shoulders turn at 90 degrees to the spine angle, which is quite easy if you have previously established the correct posture at the address position.

Golfers who habitually top the ball usually adopt an inadequate posture even before they swing the club. Most bend too far from

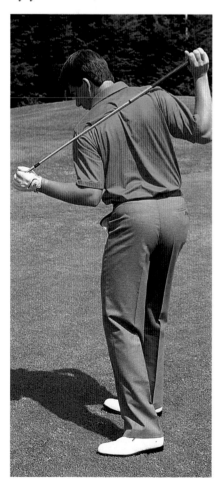

The spine angle must remain constant throughout the swing if the clubhead is to strike the ball solidly. To isolate this action and practise it, place a shaft behind your shoulders and adopt your normal posture. Notice how the left shoulder moves partially underneath the chin and the shaft points to the ground some 10 feet (3 m) ahead. In the corresponding position the other side, the right shoulder replaces the left, moving under the chin.

✔ CORRECT ✔

Left: The ideal address position posture from which you will be able to turn the body most easily in the backswing. Notice that the head is away from the chest to allow the necessary space for this shoulder turn.

✗ INCORRECT ✗

Right: Often a golfer is told to keep their head down. This usually follows a series of topped shots, the idea being that the closer the head is to the ball, the less likely the player is to strike the top of it. However, bury the chin torward the body and you will restrict the swing. Keep your chin up, not your head down.

✔ CORRECT ✔

The SEQUENCE to the downswing movements will dictate how the clubhead returns for impact. A free swinging action of the arms will promote clubhead speed and also return the full radius to the swing at impact, so striking the very back of the ball. This is confirmed in the position almost three-quarters into the through swing. Notice that the right shoulder has moved under the chin. The spine angle has been maintained through impact and beyond, and will lift only for the completion of the follow-through.

the hips or at the knees, almost invariably because they have been told to keep their head down until the ball has gone. This advice causes more topped shots than it cures. An effective posture positions the upper body so that it can turn freely on each side of the swing. The head *must* be kept up with the chin clear of your chest if you are to turn correctly. If you lower your head in an attempt to see the ball better or to stay down on the shot longer, all you achieve is a

restricted backswing turn, which may lead to lifting of the upper body to find the freedom to turn. This lifting of the body alters your spine angle and causes the topped shot. I have NEVER seen anyone lift their head up too early and top their shot as a result.

Golfers with this error will tend to lift their upper body too early, making the spine angle nearer vertical and moving the swing center upwards. This will return the clubhead to the top of the ball.

Another common fault is trying to 'muscle' the ball forwards, ap-

✗ INCORRECT ✗

A poor downswing sequence often starts with the larger muscles in the shoulders becoming active too early, the player feeling as though he is hitting the ball more powerfully. The right shoulder has moved away from its correct position, forcing the spine angle to lift and the ball to be topped. This loss of posture is seen more easily in the through swing with the right shoulder having moved around instead of UNDERNEATH the chin.

plying too much physical effort to achieve clubhead speed. Established golfers know that a powerful swing

relies far more on swing technique and how accurately you apply the clubhead to the back of the ball than it does on physical force and muscular strength. The novice has to learn this fact and cannot realistically be expected to swing smoothly when the golf hole is several hundred yards away. Everyone must experience the surprising distance the ball will travel resulting from a relatively slow swing, one which is controllable and does not thrust your shoulders round too quickly in a vain effort to hit the ball further.

Maintaining Swing Radius

The left arm should be comfortably extended at the address position while the right elbow is softer, folded in slightly towards your body. The left arm must return to this measured radius at impact for the shot to be solidly struck. What you must *not* do is to keep either arm rigidly straight; this is unnatural and cannot be maintained from address to impact. A golf swing which forces the arms to buckle will almost invariably make the clubhead strike the top of the ball. The completed swing must create a free-swinging motion of the clubhead, allowing it to move smoothly and without any steering through impact and beyond. Excessive tension is the enemy that destroys this freewheeling down and through the ball.

Initially it takes practice to ensure your left arm returns correctly extended for impact. But a weighted clubhead moving around a swing center exerts considerable centrifugal force and you should use this to your advantage. Feel how the relatively heavy clubhead wants to move in a constant orbit or arc around the body, maintaining its plane until it strikes the back of the ball solidly every time. Centrifugal force will therefore tend to pull the arms into their correctly extended, seemingly rather straight position for impact, so preventing any inclination on your part to pull inwards prior to the ball strike.

Heavy Or Fat Shots

The golf ball should be struck cleanly when the clubhead is about to complete its descent or is travelling parallel to the ground. In the first case, the slightly descending blow results in a divot being removed from the turf immediately on the target side of the ball. (Even with this descending blow, the loft of the clubface is perfectly adequate to get the ball into the air.) A heavy or fat shot hits the ground before hitting the ball, resulting in the flight being reduced in varying degrees of severity. The sole of a wooden club will probably bounce off the ground and still move the ball forward a reasonable distance, but a fat shot with an iron club will cut the turf and kill the clubhead speed, the ball often travelling only a few yards.

This error is less serious than topping because the clubhead is at least attempting to brush the ground – though in the wrong place. Start by reviewing exactly where the ball should be located in your stance. For most golfers, the lowest point in the arc will be the point on the turf immediately below the left side of your head, which is slightly left of center in your stance, but not quite opposite your left foot. Take practice swings to confirm this, noting where your divots start. In the downswing there must be a weight transference from one foot to the other in the direction you are swinging the club. As you begin the backswing the weight shifts to your right side, and for your follow-through it ends up almost entirely on your left side, the right toe remaining as the only balance point. Golfers who hit heavy shots usually do so because they fail to move the body weight correctly. For the novice, it's not so easy to trust the clubface loft to put the ball into the air. However, any attempt to lift the ball into the air by falling back just prior to impact will cause the club to strike turf well behind the ball. This is easy enough to eradicate if you set about it logically on the practice ground to move with the direction of the armswing. Complete each follow-through and check that the weight has fully transferred to your left side. Learn to trust the loft angle of the club. To assist you in the initial stages, practise with a well-lofted club, such as an 8 or 9 iron.

The generous loft angle will ensure height and encourage you to still transfer the weight, building confidence in the change of swing technique. Progress only gradually to less lofted clubs.

The second way in which a golfer will repeatedly hit the ground before hitting the ball is

Impact with an iron club should produce a slightly descending strike, hitting the ball and removing a shallow divot immediately after *(left)*. With the ball positioned just left of center in the stance, it is essential that the weight be mostly on the left side at impact. The golfer who continually hits the ground before the ball *(right)* will most commonly leave the weight on the right side, the head clearly staying too far behind.

One of the most obvious checks to make is to ensure the follow-through is complete and the weight some 90% on the left side *(below left)*. The right knee has fully moved across to encourage this weight shift, pulling the heel from the ground. Compare this to a frequently seen follow-through of golfers who hit heavy shots *(below right)*. The weight has not really shifted onto the left side and the upper body is too far to the player's right.

another result of poor body posture at the address position or a loss of posture mid-swing. An effective posture enables you to stand tall even though the upper body is angled slightly forwards from the hips. From this posture you can turn freely to either side without altering the swing center. But if the posture is incorrect or changes in mid-swing, the impact will be affected. The most common error is to angle the upper body excessively, which forces the player to stand further away from the ball. The player tends to fall forwards because the swing lacks balance, and as a consequence is almost bound to hit the ground first.

The spine angle must remain constant throughout the swing in order to strike the back of the ball consistently. As the downswing begins, the left arm and right shoulder must separate as part of the correct sequence of movements *(above left)*. However, should the right shoulder drop early in the downswing *(above right)*, the center of the swing will move closer to the ball. This will in turn cause the club to strike the ground considerably before the ball. This is an error better golfers fall into should they work excessively at 'driving' the legs in order to increase power.

Correct this by establishing a better address position posture, encouraging the upper body to be taller and the ball nearer to you.

CHECKPOINTS

○ The ball position must coincide with a point opposite the left side of your head, or left of center in the stance.

○ Check that you incorporate a shift of weight in the direction that the club swings, with particular emphasis on the follow-through position.

○ Develop these ideas with a lofted club that inspires confidence, such as an 8 or 9 iron.

○ If your problems persist, review your address position and ensure that you have an effective posture which keeps the upper body sitting up rather than falling forwards.

Skying

Affecting only the wooden clubs, skying occurs when only the upper edge of the clubhead and the top of the clubface fully contacts the ball. The ball compresses inwards at impact and effectively wraps around the angle between the top edge and hitting face to dictate its trajectory. The ball is sent very high into the air, losing the normal low trajectory we associate with the wooden clubs.

✔ CORRECT ✔

Impact with a driver from a teeing ground. The club must approach the back of the ball on a shallow path, ideally ascending a touch at the point of impact. Although the weight is mostly on the left side, the head has not shifted forwards and the hands are above or fractionally leading the clubface.

Many golfers who sky shots look immediately to the height of tee peg they use and lower this, but the answer rarely lies only there. Consider exactly what must be happening at impact for the top edge of the clubhead to be able to direct the ball skywards. The downswing must be too steep, with the hands well ahead of the clubface. This tilts the shaft forwards excessively, reduces the effective loft on the clubface and introduces the top edge. In addition, the swing is descending too steeply at impact. A tee shot with a wooden club is most effective when the sole of the club is travelling parallel to the ground or is slightly ascending at impact. A golfer who hits skied drives is clearly hitting down instead of through the ball.

Once faulty impact factors have been identified, swing errors can more easily be isolated. Golfers who sky shots also tend to slice, pull, top and hit fat shots and tend to be inconsistent with their shotmaking generally. Check your address position first. The ball should be to the left of center in the stance, with your weight just favouring the right side to promote

✘ INCORRECT ✘

Skying the shot is due to the hands leading the clubhead at impact, the upper body usually far forwards of ideal too as shown here. These errors cause the clubhead to descend steeply prior to impact, introducing the possibility of the top edge of the wooden club directing the shot high and lacking distance.

a slightly ascending strike at impact. If the ball was more torward the right foot or the weight too much on the left leg, the club would still be descending at impact.

Next, check your shoulder alignment and overall swing shape. An address position with the shoulders 'open', facing slightly to the left of the target, will promote a swing which moves across the target-line at impact, from 'outside-to-inside'. This swing shape tends to be steeper than normal, and may acount for the clubhead to be still descending at impact. Shoulder alignment

✗ INCORRECT ✗
This address position shows the two common address position errors which could lead to skying. Firstly, the golf ball is right of center, at which point in the downswing the clubhead will still be descending. Secondly, the weight is mostly on the left side, which will aggravate the steepness in the downswing.

CHECKPOINTS

○ Skying is caused by the club steeply descending into impact instead of the base of the swing being more shallow or flat-bottomed.

○ For tee shots, the club should be slightly ascending at impact to maximize distance. Keep the ball positioned left of center and your weight favouring the right side at the address position.

○ Check your shoulder line and overall swing shape, preferring the club to approach impact from around the body on the inside path.

○ Most golfers who sky shots do so because the hands are excessively ahead of the hitting face at impact, so tilting the clubhead forwards and introducing the top edge.

○ If the wrists are encouraged to unfold or release for impact, the face of the club will strike the back of the ball solidly as the swing shallows out.

could be correct at the address position, but if you fail to turn adequately in the backswing or cast the right shoulder out early into the downswing, the swing can still be from outside-to-inside, moving to the left of target in the hitting area.

The largest category of golfers who sky shots will combine one or more of these address position or basic swing errors, with the hands arriving at impact too far ahead of the clubhead. This has the effect of opening the clubface, which is why there is a tendency to slice shots, too. Assuming the address position achieves normal ball positioning,

✔ CORRECT ✔
Check that the golf ball is correctly positioned in relation to the feet. It should appear no further back than some four inches (10 cm) inside the left heel. In addition, encourage an ascending strike by placing the weight favouring the right side.

✔ CORRECT ✔

Check that your address position permits you to swing the club so that it approaches the ball from around the body prior to impact. Particular emphasis should be placed on the shoulder alignment, here shown to be square.

square shoulders and good weight distribution, you have only to look to a couple of swing error possibilities. If you swing from the 'inside' path, with the club approaching impact from around the body, and let the wrists unfold or 'release' in time, the swing will shallow out. Such a shallow arc through the hitting area will present the clubface solidly into the back of the ball. Once this better swing shape is grooved into place through practise, skied shots will be eliminated.

✘ INCORRECT ✘

An open shoulder alignment *(above)* will cause the club to swing rather straight back from the ball, limiting the shoulder turn and encouraging the same shape approaching impact. Such a swing will be too steep, descending at impact instead of slightly ascending.

✘ INCORRECT ✘

Left: A typical halfway down position for a golfer who skies the ball. The shaft should be parallel to the line of the toes at this point, but is well outside this. The club can only descend steeply at impact, either topping it completely or going underneath it and sending the ball very high.

Shanking

There can be few problems in golf so discouraging as the shank, and those who hit this shot more than occasionally would argue that it is the most soul-destroying mis-hit of them all. The shanked shot, or socket, occurs when the ball is struck by the combination of clubface and circular hosel at the bottom end of the shaft of an iron club. If very bad it may even be struck by the hosel alone. This shot cannot occur with a wooden club because the design does not incorporate a rounded hosel. The equivalent wood shot, struck by the neck of the club, sends the ball low to the left. The shank is reserved for the iron clubs and the ball flies generally low and to the right. This contact problem can often affect just one part of the player's game – for example, the shorter shots into the green. It is one of those errors that may virtually disappear for a time and then, for no apparent reason, return. You either have to analyse the error yourself and set about solving it or seek the assistance of a teaching professional. I have found that if I precisely identify where the error originates in a person's swing technique, the solution can be easily found too. The correction may take a while to groove into place, replacing the old muscle-memory with the new one. I believe that the long term solutions are always contained in the very basics of the swing technique.

The dreaded shank. One of the most dramatic of all errors, the ball shooting off the socket of the clubhead to the right, almost invariably into trees or rough. It often affects pitch shots from some 40 yards (36 m) before the green as shown here.

There are just two reasons why the shank can occur: the first is related to the sliced shot, the second results from swing plane changes.

The Open Clubface Shank

If you slice a lot of golf shots and shank at least occasionally too, look to your clubface for the solution. If you typically shank pitch shots from some 30 or 40 yards (27-36 m) before the green, check this error out before you consider a further possibility.

A straight shot occurs because the clubface is square at impact and the swing path coincides with the ball-to-target-line. A sliced shot curves to the right because the

The open clubface shank is closely linked with golfers who already slice shots generally. The face returns open as shown here, the socket being the first part of the club to reach the ball. This generally accompanies a change in swing plane.

clubface is open at impact, but if the face is badly open, the striking surface becomes much narrower. The socket of the club is returned to the ball with the wrists locked up, and the ball reacts to the combination of the two. This is why golfers who slice also tend to shank some shots, the shank being an extreme version of the slice. It often affects golfers who, with pitch shots, roll their hands excessively in the backswing and fail to rotate them back before impact. As the clubface returns, there is a tendency to use the right shoulder excessively just prior to impact. This is often mistakenly assumed to be the root cause of the error. In fact, the reason the right shoulder moves

✔ CORRECT ✔
The ideal impact position shows the hands fractionally ahead of the ball, the clubface returning squarely as the downswing sequence encourages the wrists to unfold or 'release'.

around too early is because the poor action of the wrists and lower arms forces it to do so: the upper body spins round in response to the lack of armswing and correct application of the clubface.

The solution is to resist any tendency to independently roll or hinge the wrists early in the backswing. At halfway back, check that an imaginary line drawn across the leading edge of the clubface points to 11.30, and that it has not rotated the face open so that it points at 1 o'clock, for instance. As the club moves to the ball in the downswing, encourage the right hand and forearm to rotate over the left prior to the impact position, thus closing the clubface if anything. Further check this by reviewing your clubface halfway into the downswing, looking for the leading edge to point at 11.30 again or even torward the 11 o'clock position. The more you close the clubface in the swing, the less the right shoulder will move outwards just prior to striking the ball. As a result, most golfers who correct their shank will also improve or solve their slicing problem too!

Change of Swing Plane

Picture a swing moving around the body. It moves upwards as well as around the player in the backswing, returns in a similar way for impact and continues around and upwards into the follow-through. Effectively, the swing moves in a circular arc or orbit around a center pivot located at your upper chest, between the shoulders.

The orbit or swing plane is determined by the address position. The club shaft length, your body posture and the distance you stand from the ball all combine to dictate the overall shape of the swing. Imagine the swing plane as the

sloping roof of a house, angled so that it passes from the ball through your swing center and out behind and above your neck. As you set your swing in motion, the shaft will coincide with this ideal plane at each stage of the orbit. At halfway back the shaft should be parallel both to the ground and to the ball-to-target-line. At the top of your backswing the shaft should again be parallel both to the ground and to the ball-to-target-line, thus indicating that on the second half of the backswing the shaft has remained on plane. Retain this plane all the way to impact on the downswing and the back

✘ INCORRECT ✘
If the upper body unwinds too early, the right shoulder tends to move away from its normal position, throwing the club into a flatter swing plane for the downswing and shanking the ball as a result. This is accompanied by the clubface being left wide open as the wrists fail to 'release'.

A shank can occur because the clubhead returns on a flatter plane then it travelled in the backswing. Here the clubhead is square but the ball contacts both the face and the socket.

CHECKPOINTS

❍ A shank is when the socket of an iron club strikes the ball, or combines with the clubface to make contact. You cannot shank with a wooden club owing to its lack of a hosel.

❍ There are only two ways to shank a ball: leaving the clubface wide open, and swinging in a shallower plane on the downswing than on the backswing.

❍ If you tend to shank, practise pitch shots to the green, checking that the hands are not independently rolling early into the backswing.

❍ A shank is often associated with a slice, when the clubface is left wide open at impact.

❍ Review your clubface control within the swing to correct any tendency to roll the wrists in the backswing or lock the wrists prior to impact.

❍ A poor release will tend to cause the right shoulder to unwind prematurely, compounding the error by making the swing plane even more shallow.

❍ Check the first movement of your downswing to ensure the shaft drops into the ideal plane, not underneath it as the lower body slides left.

✔ CORRECT ✔
The impact position should reflect a downswing sequence which shifts the weight with the lower body and only turns the shoulders to face the target once the ball is on its way to the green.

✘ INCORRECT ✘
An impact position which will shank the ball shows how the right shoulder has turned prematurely, shallowing out the swing arc just prior to this. The right shoulder has effectively cast the clubhead further away from where it started.

of the ball will be struck solidly from the center of the clubhead.

The shank usually occurs owing to an error early in the downswing. The plane changes, causing the clubhead to move on a flatter orbit than that of the backswing. Interestingly, it need not move one specific way, as the shank can happen whether the shaft moves underneath the plane line or above it. The recovery of the club as it struggles to find the correct plane for impact forces the error. The dropping of the shaft below the plane line early in the down-

✔ CORRECT ✔
It is essential that the downswing starts off in plane, the left arm pulling downwards while the lower body begins to turn to face the golf ball. A line extending from the golf shaft would coincide with the target-line or appear just before it as shown.

✗ INCORRECT ✗
This early downswing error has dropped the shaft underneath the plane line, which shallows out the swing arc for impact and delivers the socket of the club to the ball. The right elbow has folded excessively and the left arm has not pulled down enough.

✗ INCORRECT ✗
An unwinding of the shoulders can lead to the same error at impact. The left arm has not pulled downwards enough early in the downswing which has moved the shaft outwards, away from the player. Such a shallowing out of the swing arc can dictate that the socket meets the ball.

swing is more closely associated with better golfers. These players are often taught to hit from the inside path, with the clubhead approaching more from around the body to deliver a very solid strike and maximize clubhead speed. If the hips do not recover control of the club for impact the clubhead continues to move away from the body, crossing from inside-to-outside the ball-to-target-line at the point of impact. The clubhead's orbit becomes too shallow just prior to impact, so that the socket rather than the clubface meets the ball.

The opposite error can produce the same shot. If the upper body, particularly the right shoulder, moves round too soon in the down-swing, the shaft is seen to be above the plane line when viewed from behind. This swing orbit has al-

Try an exercise which will promote the downward pulling action of the arms, instead of them moving away from the body at some stage in the downswing. Start with the clubhead beyond a golf ball but return to hit the shot in the normal way.

ready become too shallow owing to the effect of that turn of the upper body, tending to cast the armswing outwards rather than downwards

and delivering the socket of the club to the ball instead of the hitting face.

The solution lies in your practising moving the club through the correct swing reference points until this occurs automatically when playing the shot. Look particularly at your first movement down: while the shaft will possibly move slightly under the plane line early on, it should have recovered to be parallel to the ball-to-target-line halfway down. There is one other way to help you feel what a steeper downswing will be like. Form your address position with the clubhead resting beyond the ball by some 4 in (10 cm). Swing to three-quarters length and hit the golf ball. The feeling is that the arms have to pull inwards to make the solid contact.

Directional Errors

Full shots require both directional control and distance. While problems with either can cause you to score badly, it is better to keep the ball reasonably straight and in play rather than hitting it further but all over the course. The inaccurate golfer will always struggle to hold a score together over 18 holes, whereas the shorter but more accurate hitter will at least be able to find the ball and play his next shot from the mown fairway or, at worst, the light rough. Directional errors fall into four categories, but before we consider them, you need to understand a few points about the moment of impact

and why the ball flies in a particular way. If you watch the flight of the golf ball you can learn a lot about the kind of impact that occurred. The fact is that so many established golfers clearly have little or no concept of what causes their inaccurate golf ball flight, so what chance do they ever stand of making the correction? It might sort itself out by chance or you might stumble across an idea after hours of experimentation, but most often a solution is only temporary until you more precisely pinpoint the error and correct it. It is surprising the length of time many golfers will persevere with swing errors without

seeking the assistance and knowledge of a teaching professional who can isolate one specific fault and save the player a lot of time and fruitless effort.

Golf is a game of clubface control, and the flight characteristics of the ball are principally dictated by this. The precise direction in which the clubhead travels at im-

The sliced shot is very common amongst novice golfers. The shots tend to be inaccurate, inconsistent and they lack distance. They tend to affect less lofted clubs more, such as the driver, because there is less backspin to hide the sidespin which produces the curved flight.

pact is influential, but I would emphasize that 75 per cent of directional control is achieved through the clubface position. There is one other factor which influences direction, particularly with the woods, and that is how well you contact the ball, especially if the ball is struck with the toe or heel of the clubface.

A clubface can be 'square' at impact, so producing a straight flight, 'open', which will cause the ball to curve away to the right in the air or 'closed' which would make it curve left. However, the type of club used can influence this, because the amount of backspin produced greatly affects the amount the ball curves. If you hit a shot solidly with a wedge or 9 iron the backspin will be so great that it will largely override the effect of sidespin. However, an identical error with a long iron or wood will see the ball curve badly once the initial velocity has dissipated and reduced backspin rate can no longer inhibit the effect of sidespin. The ball might finish 30 or 40 yards (27-36m) off target. But don't be misled into believing the error exists only with the less lofted clubs. In almost every case the error is consistent across all clubs and is due to a fault in your swing which must be identified, understood and corrected through patient and constructive practice.

Correcting The Slice

The sliced shot curves out of control to the right in the air. It tends to be a poor golfer's error, and it is very inaccurate, inconsistent and lacks distance. This shot is quite different from the fade which, by comparison, curves the ball under control slightly from left to right. The slice is a very common error with newcomers to the sport, and once grooved into place, it usually requires a considerable effort to correct it. One of the problems is making sure that the shoulders are parallel with the ball-to-target-line, and unless you learn how to eradicate misalignment from the moment you take up golf, this error will become a habit. An 'open' position, facing left of the target, makes it difficult to swing the club on a path around the body in the backswing, and can affect how the wrists control the clubface.

The root of the problem is the clubface position. However, in order to begin to correct this, you must first develop a sound address position routine. How you aim the clubface, grip the club and how squarely you stand all influence your swing and it's not possible to work at correcting the faulty clubface alignment until you adopt an address position which allows you to turn the body and swing correctly.

Check your grip. By raising your left hand you should see two complete knuckles and half of a third. A grip associated with an open clubface would show only one or one and a half knuckles, so as the hand reverted to its natural position just before impact, the clubface would open. Your right thumb should ride over your left, covering it from view, while the right palm faces the target. A right-hand grip which folds the hand over too far (to the left of neutral as you look down on it) is likely to open the clubface at impact as it reverts to its more natural position. Check the remainder of your address position, with the emphasis on the squareness of the shoulders, hips, knees and toes.

There are various check points in the swing which you will need to review. Take the club back and stop at halfway, with the shaft parallel to the ground. An imaginary line drawn across the leading edge of the clubface should point at 11.30 on a clock face. But if you have rolled the face open by hing-

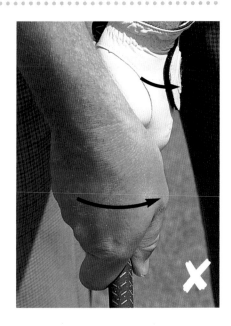

✗ INCORRECT ✗
One of the initial checks must be the grip. The hands always try to find their natural position for impact so if either the left, the right or both hands are placed incorrectly to begin with, this alone could cause the slice. Here, both hands are to the player's left of neutral, the left hand showing barely one knuckle, the right forced too far over.

ing or rotating the wrists, the clubface will point more at 1 o'clock. The top of the backswing should reflect how correct the clubface position is halfway back, so it is less important to check once the club has passed out of sight behind and above you.

At halfway into the downswing, again with the shaft horizontal, check that the face has returned to its neutral position and is not left open.

If everything is correct so far, you can conclude that the error occurs just prior to impact. Many golfers who slice the ball fail at this very last stage, yet surprisingly few recognize this error and therefore fail to correct it until the slice is grooved into place. Remember that your hands and lower arms must rotate anti-clockwise at the same time as your body turns through to face the target. This crossing over is termed 'release' and describes how the wrists must unfold immediately prior to impact in order to square off the clubface. The most common reason why golfers slice is that the wrists partially lock up and fail to rotate through the hitting area. At the point of impact the hands are too far in front of the clubhead and the clubface stays open, carving the ball away to the right.

✗ INCORRECT ✗
An open clubface is the reason for the curved flight. At impact the clubface is angled to the right, partially dictating that the ball starts out in that direction, but mostly causing the curvature on the shot once the initial power has reduced.

The correction is easily made once you have learned to control the clubface position and grow accustomed to the correct action of your wrists and lower arms. A good release involves the feeling of the right hand rotating over the left once the club has reached hip height in the downswing. If your wrists work independently or too quickly, you will close the clubface and hook the shot to the left. If you partially lock you wrists the face remains open. The neutral position which will give the vital square clubface at impact must move the face from its 11.30 position at halfway down to 11.30 again once the shaft is horizontal in the

✔ CORRECT ✔
This is an excellent impact position, the clubface having squared up just prior to striking the ball. The hands are marginally in front of the ball. The left arm and shaft appearing to form a fairly straight line.

through swing. Learn this in a mini-swing and it is quite easy to incorporate it later in the full swing. By practising a mini-swing you can isolate the error and correct it more easily. Remember that the wrists cannot unfold effectively if your grip pressure is too tight, so ensure you hold the club in such a way that the release happens naturally.

Although a slice which simply curves away to the right of target can be solved quite easily, the more established golfer will probably have tried to compensate for his error by aiming to the left, or he may have adjusted his swing shape to hide its effect. The latter usually takes the form of an independent

✗ INCORRECT ✗
This is a typical slicer's impact position. The wrists are too far ahead of the clubhead, opening the clubface and causing the shot to curve away to the right. The more the wrists lead at impact, the greater the tendency to slice the shot.

✔ CORRECT ✔

The correct downswing sequence will encourage the right wrist and lower arm to rotate over the left throughout the hitting area. This can be judged by the direction in which the toe end points at halfway through. A square clubface at impact results in the toe end being directly upwards at the position shown.

✘ INCORRECT ✘

If the lower arms and wrists fail to rotate enough throughout the hitting area, the clubface will stay open and slice the golf ball away to the right. This faulty clubface can be easily seen at halfway through. This error is the most common reason why many golfers slice the ball.

CHECKPOINTS

○ A sliced shot curves away to the right owing to sidespin caused by an 'open' clubface at impact.

○ The slice will be more pronounced with less lofted clubs, particularly the woods, because there is relatively little backspin to control the direction of flight.

○ Your grip should show two and a half knuckles on the left hand, when viewed from the front.

○ The palm of the right hand must face the target at the address position and again at impact. A right hand grip causing a slice would be too far to the player's left at the set-up.

○ Avoid rolling the wrists independently early in the backswing, as this will 'open' the clubface.

○ Check that the leading edge is at 11.30 on a clock face halfway into the downswing.

○ Rotate the right hand over the left throughout the hitting area at the same time as the body turns through.

○ Most golfers who slice lock their wrists and lower arms prior to impact.

○ The outside-to-inside swing direction contributes to the slice, but its prime cause is an 'open' clubface.

turn of the shoulders too early in the downswing, altering the path of the club as it passes through impact. The shot is then directed to the left before it curves back onto target as the effect of sidespin takes over. Some golfers wrongly believe that swing direction is what causes the slice, as it glances across the back of the ball in the way a table tennis ball is given a sideways spin. However, in golf the position of the clubface is most important and you can work at improving the swing direction only after clubface control has been achieved.

Correcting The Hook

A hook is a shot that curves out of control from right to left. It is quite different from the 'draw', which is more controlled and is often chosen by better golfers as a preferred shape of shot. The hook is caused by the clubface contacting the ball while in a 'closed' position – that is, turned to the left of the target. A ball which hooks tends to fly lower and run further on landing owing to the club's reduced loft

The hooked shot curves out of control to the left in flight. Although not as weak in flight as the slice, it can be very inaccurate as it tends to bounce and roll into trouble due to its lower flight. Many golfers who anticipate a hook will aim away to the right to compensate.

at impact as a result of the face being closed. You can see this clearly for yourself by closing the clubface, angling the face to the left of the target. A hook shot usually travels a considerable distance, but it will obviously be inaccurate and difficult to control when you are playing to a green which requires a more lofted, softer-landing shot.

Significantly fewer golfers hook than slice because this error is more associated with the wrists and lower arms being too active before the club makes contact with the ball. But that is just one of several reasons why a hooked shot may occur, and you should check a number of points to establish the cause of your hook.

You should look at the clubface at the address position to confirm

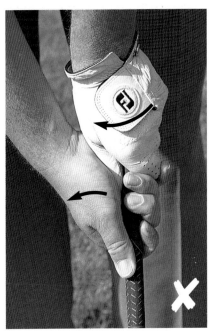

✗ INCORRECT ✗
The most obvious place to look first for an error is in the grip. A typical grip adopted by a golfer who hooks will position one or both hands to the player's right of neutral. Here the left hand shows all four knuckles and the palm of the right hand is mostly underneath the shaft, instead of facing the target.

✗ INCORRECT ✗

A closed clubface at impact causes the hooked shot. If the face is turned to the left of target, the ball will have sidespin imparted which will cause the ball to turn left once the initial velocity has reduced.

that it is square, not turned to the left, before you begin the swing. Pay great attention to your grip, as most hooked shots are the product of poor positioning of the hands. The correct placement of the left hand, as we have seen, will show just two and a half knuckles from the front. You can check this by looking into a mirror or raising the shaft upwards until you can look down on your own hands. A grip associated with hooking will show

✔ CORRECT ✔

The ideal position of the clubface at halfway in to the backswing will direct a line drawn across the leading edge to 11.30 on an imaginary clock face. This involves the wrists hinging just slightly as the shaft nears horizontal.

✗ INCORRECT ✗

The golfer who hooks the ball often closes the clubface at this position, a line drawn across the leading edge directed at about 10.00 on an imaginary clock face. The wrists have failed to hinge in response to the shoulder turn.

three or even four knuckles. However, correcting a hooker's grip is initially uncomfortable for many golfers, so you may find it takes a little time to correct this error. Sometimes it is the right hand alone which causes the clubface to turn in. If this hand is too far to the player's right on the club, in too 'strong' a position, it will tend to revert to a more natural position at impact, closing the face and

causing the ball to hook. The right hand must be positioned so that its palm faces the target. This is easily achieved if you open the hand out and then re-grip once you are satisfied that the palm has not rotated around to your right.

Assuming your aim and grip are both correct, you will have to look to your swing technique to straighten up the ball flight. Remember that the clubface must move through reference points in the swing, those stationary positions where you are able to identify any error and rectify it. Halfway into your backswing, with the shaft parallel to the ground, a line across the leading edge of the clubface should point at the 11.30 position, but if the face is closed, the line will

point more torward 10 on the imaginary clock. This error so early in the swing is due to the wrists failing to hinge and the right elbow moving away from the body instead of folding torward the hip.

A closed clubface at the top of the backswing will be directed torward the sky. However, the key to a neutral or square position at the top of the swing is how correct the face is halfway back, as the full

✔ CORRECT ✔
At halfway into the through swing, the toe end of the club should point skywards. This is a result of the correct lower arm and wrist action prior to impact. An imaginary line drawn across the clubface will point at the 11.30 position as the player sees it.

✗ INCORRECT ✗
Should the wrists roll over excessively prior to impact, the clubface will turn into a closed position, hooking the shot to the left. This will be noticed if you stop the club halfway through, the toe end pointing behind the player and only slightly skywards.

backswing tends to always be an extension of the smaller one.

Halfway into the downswing, the neutral clubface should again point at the 11.30 position, but a closed face is directed more toward the ground. From here onwards, you must resist the tendency of the right hand and forearm to rotate prematurely over the left, as this will snap the clubface closed and cause the ball to hook. Instead, feel the back of the left hand pull through with the clubhead always trailing the arms and wrists. In addition turn the lower body, especially the hips, to create the space for the arms to pull through. Really push the right knee through until it meets the left leg at the completion of the follow-through. You can check your positioning in the forward swing by holding the club shaft at horizontal and confirming the correct toe-end up position. A closed clubface will have rolled over and once again will face more toward the ground, or at 10 o'clock.

Most golfers who have grooved this error into place will have found a method of compensation which allows them to at least dis-

guise the problem on the course and play reasonably well. They will either aim to the right of target and let the curvature of the shot bring the ball back to the fairway, or will develop a swing shape which directs the ball down the right side of the hole before it swings back onto target. Either way, the error and compensation make a very difficult balancing act, one which is very likely to collapse periodically. Poor aim is easily corrected by taking more care with alignment when practising. However if your swing is moving from inside-to-outside through impact, when the clubface position is corrected the ball will fly straight to the right – a 'push' shot. So remember to correct the faulty clubface setting as well as your swing direction, bearing in mind that golf is principally a game of clubface control.

Set aside some time to practise the corrected swing, but initially on the practise ground or golf range, not the course. It is very likely that the new positions in the swing and your overall impression of it will be discomfort, but this eases as you progress.

CHECKPOINTS

○ A hooked shot is caused by the clubface being 'closed' at impact, imparting sidespin which makes the ball curve off target to the left.

○ The ball will generally fly lower and run a considerable distance.

○ Check that your left hand is in the neutral position. A grip associated with the hook will show three and probably all four knuckles on the left hand.

○ The palm of the right hand must face the target. If it is positioned more under the club, the clubface will 'close' at impact.

○ Check the clubface halfway into the downswing: if it is in a 'closed' position it will point at 10.00 on the imaginary clock face, whereas it should point at 11.30.

○ Throughout the hitting area, resist any tendency of the right hand to roll over the left. Try instead to keep the back of the left hand directed at the target until past impact.

○ If you also swing from 'inside-to-outside' through the hitting area, remember that this is your compensation for the probability of the ball curving badly to the left in flight.

Correcting The Pull

A 'pulled' shot flies straight but to the left of the target. It tends to fly the full distance but usually on a slightly lower than normal trajectory. The ball starts to the left of target because the clubhead is travelling in that direction at the moment of impact. In addition, the clubface must be also angled to the left of the target, otherwise the ball would tend to curve back toward the target in flight. The easiest way to understand the error is to recall exactly

what should happen in a good swing.

Imagine a clock face placed around you at hip height. 12 o'clock is straight ahead in front of your eyes, directly opposite you. Its center is just in front of your belt buckle. 3 o'clock is to your right. 9 o'clock is in the direction of the target. At halfway in the downswing, the shaft should pass through the 3 o'clock position, then continue until it coincides with the ball-to-target-line at the exact

moment of impact, and then move into the 9 o'clock position in the forward swing. This elliptical shape of the swing through impact will move the clubhead on a gentle arc approaching from around the body. In the impact area it travels down the target line before continuing around the body in the follow-through.

A shot is pulled when the shaft moves through the 2 o'clock position halfway in the downswing, passes impact while moving to

✗ INCORRECT ✗
The pulled shot can occur because the shoulders fail to turn enough in the backswing. Here the shaft is badly 'laid off', pointing left of target because the shoulders have turned only 60 degrees. Unless the downswing re-routes, the shape of swing will cause a ball flight to the left.

✗ INCORRECT ✗
Halfway into the downswing the shaft is approaching from the 2 o'clock position on the clock face. It should be parallel to the target-line. This position is often described as 'outside' and as the downswing continues the shaft will move across the line to finish 'inside'.

✗ INCORRECT ✗
The corresponding position at halfway through, the shaft now significantly to the left of the target when it should be parallel to the line of the toes. The ball flight will be to the left, assuming the clubface is directed that way too.

the left of the target and continues through to 8 o'clock in the forward swing. It occurs because the shoulders unwind prematurely in the downswing when the player fails to pull downwards sufficiently with the arms. The shape of swing is usually referred to as 'outside-to-inside' because it has moved from outside the ideal shape to inside it.

To correct this swing shape, the most effective way is to work at developing a touch of the opposite error initially, promoting the correct feeling in the swing and probably accelerating the learning process too. Imagine that the shaft must move through the 3.30 position at halfway into the downswing, achieved by resisting the premature turning of the right shoulder and instead promoting the left arm to

pull more downwards. This first part of the downswing will doubtless need practice to familiarize yourself with such an alien movement, but the more you develop the correct sequence from early in the downswing, the easier it becomes to repeat when actually hitting shots. Feel how the clubhead seems to move out to the right of target a touch at the moment of impact and the shaft points to the 9.30 position on the clock face. The shaft will seem to continue toward the target past impact. Remember that the shape of the swing is dictated primarily by how you move the club in this mini-swing, and that you need place less importance on the top of the backswing and follow-through as these respond to a better swing shape throughout the hitting area.

CHECKPOINTS

○ A pulled shot flies straight but to the left of the target. It is caused by a combination of the swing moving from 'outside-to-inside' plus a clubface which also faces left.

○ Initially, work at a slight over-correction, so accelerating the learning process.

○ The faulty swing direction moves the shaft from 2 o'clock to 8 o'clock on your imaginary guide, the center of this clock being just in front of your waist.

○ Most often the pull is caused by the upper body unwinding prematurely in the downswing. Replace this over-use of the right shoulder with the feeling of the left arm pulling downwards more vigorously.

○ Feel that the clubhead swings out toward the target in the forward swing.

Correcting The Push

The 'pushed' shot starts to the right of the target and continues in that direction, with no curve in the flight. The shot tends to fly a touch higher than normal and achieves full or nearly full distance. The push is mainly associated with golfers who also hook the ball, the primary difference being the clubface position at impact. For the shot to be pushed, the swing must be moving from inside-to-outside through the hitting area, but the clubface must also be angled that way, in a slightly open position. If the face was square to the target, the shot would curve from right to left in the air, which is a hook, not a push. However, a player who hooks will usually compensate by moving the clubhead on this inside-to-outside path. On the occasions that the clubface returns open instead of closed, the effects of the compensation are to push the shot to the right of target.

You will most easily identify the error and its correction by referring to the swing model explained in the last section about pulling. The shaft should be parallel to the ball-to-target-line at halfway down, or pointing torward the 3 o'clock on the clock face. The pushed shot will be caused by the shaft dropping excessively underneath the plane line early in the downswing, most often because the player moves his hips and legs directly torward the target, causing the right shoulder to drop and force the elbow to tuck in too

✗ INCORRECT ✗
An overuse of the shoulders in the backswing will cause the shaft to cross over at the top. The error is nearly always very early in the backswing, but the most likely shape for this downswing is 'inside' the ideal line, pushing the shot to the right.

✗ INCORRECT ✗
This downswing has dropped the shaft to the 4 o'clock position, the hips not facing the ball as they should be doing and the shoulders are still turned too much to the player's right.

✗ INCORRECT ✗
Following a poor start to the downswing the only direction in which the club can swing is to the right of target, and if the clubface is also facing that way, the shot will be 'pushed'.

CHECKPOINTS

○ A pushed shot flies straight but to the right of the target. It will also tend to fly a touch higher than normal and achieve a reasonable distance.

○ The swing direction is from 'inside-to-out-side' but the clubface must also be angled to the right, or 'square' to the swing direction.

○ Initially, work at a slight over-correction as this will accelerate the learning process.

○ The faulty direction will move the shaft through 4 o'clock at halfway down, swinging out to 10 o'clock at halfway through. Offset this by turning the upper body earlier into the downswing until the shaft finds the 2.30 position on the clock face. From here, the swing direction will feel as though it is moving across the body to the left of target.

much. This will direct the shaft more toward the 4 o'clock position, after which the clubhead is forced to travel from inside-to-outside through impact, the shaft continuing into the forward swing until it passes through the 10 o'clock position.

The correction involves identifying exactly where you must be at halfway into the downswing. Try to exaggerate the correction slightly to accelerate learning it, and move the shaft through the 2.30 position, feeling how the right shoulder must rotate outwards

rather than drop downwards early in the downswing. Following this, feel the swing move a touch to the left of target at impact and continue until the shaft coincides with the 8.30 position at halfway through. Don't place too much importance on the top of the backswing and follow-through because they tend to adjust automatically in response to the mini-swing, the half length movement to hip height either side. Once you have practised and feel more comfortable with this adjustment, you should amend the swing to find the neutral shape.

INDEX